Share the Irresistible Story of Jesus

By J. David Eshleman

ChurchSmart
RESOURCES

Published by ChurchSmart Resources

We are an evangelical Christian publisher committed to producing excellent products at affordable prices to help church leaders accomplish effective ministry in the areas of church planting, church growth, church renewal and leadership development.

All Scripture quoted is New International Version unless otherwise noted.

For a free catalog of our resources call 1-800-253-4276.
Visit us at **www.ChurchSmart.com**

Cover design by: Robert Rummel
Edited by: Phil Newell

Copyright © 2016

ISBN: 978-1-936812-20-2

Dedication

To Jesus, who made it possible for me to have the joy of relating to many people during my more than half-a-century of pastoral ministry.

To my wife Helen
without whom I could not have written this book. Her prayers, loving support, helpful suggestions and long hours of proofreading were a constant source of encouragement.

To those who read my previous book, *Now Go Forward: Reaching Out to Grow Your Congregation.* Their reports, along with the Holy Spirit's persistent urging, enabled me to write this book.

Acknowledgments

I am grateful to God and to the many people who have been part of my life making this work possible. My experience in pastoring growing congregations and church planting over fifty years in both rural and urban congregations has blessed me beyond measure. The past six years, I have had the privilege of ministering as a church consultant to approximately seventy congregations. With this background, I present this work praying that the lessons and truths I am learning will inspire multitudes to both live and share Jesus to those they meet.

Most of all I am greatly indebted to my wife, Helen, for her persistent prayer ministry for this work, her time and effort in proofreading, her timely corrections, and for tolerating the many hours when I closed myself off in the study.
Betsy Cacciola's suggestions and proofreading have also added much to this document. Special thanks to David Wetzler and the staff at ChurchSmart Resources for their encouragement and helpful suggestions.

You'll find this material adapts well to individual enrichment, to small group study and to leadership teams in your congregation. It speaks directly to Christians who want to share the Good News and to small congregations struggling to reach their communities for Christ.

Jesus said, "I will build my church." I offer this book to Him to be used for His glory.

Contents

Preface

The Great Commission is the mission statement of the church. The Church has one main reason to exist: to make disciples who make disciples. The church exists for the benefit of non-members. As Louis Palou has said, "The church is like manure. Pile it together and it stinks; spread it out and it encircles the world."

The typical "Christian" in the United States has not spread it out. Only six percent of Christians attempt to give a verbal witness to their faith. They may give token gifts to missions, but only a very few have taken the Great Commission seriously for themselves. They feel little or no responsibility or necessity to share the Good News.

My purpose is to motivate Christians and churches to make the Great Commission the compelling passion of their lives and churches. Every church has implied in their vision/purpose statement, written or unwritten, their intention to obey Jesus' Great Commission. But somehow the Great Commission gets lost in the many activities and programs of the church. Today, persons can be active, respected members of a congregation and yet never make an attempt to lead another person to Christ. The Great Commission is not on their radar screen. Others are frozen with fear at the thought of sharing Jesus.

A healthy church will be driven by the Great Commission and function by the Great Commandment. If we make it our priority to obey Jesus' commands, our lives and our churches will resemble a hospital emergency room where people are healed, receive new hope and go out to make disciples who make disciples.

My passion is to help Christians raise their level of compassion for those who are lost. Sharing the Good News and making disciples is the most important responsibility the church and its members have been given. We must be courageous and sensitive to God-given opportunities to live and to share the Good News. Our greatest obstacle is not cognitive information about our mission but a lack of zeal and faith to carry out what we know Jesus commands us to do.

My prayer is that all followers of Jesus realize that their primary calling is to move out under the Holy Spirit's power to push back the gates of hell. (Matt. 16:18). Taking Jesus' final words seriously will help us to mature as disciples. Making disciples removes our lethargy to pray and study God's Word in order to become equipped to disciple others.

When Christ is our life, sharing Jesus becomes as natural as breathing. The supernatural becomes natural. (Col. 3:1-3).

Scripture references are from the New International Version unless indicated otherwise. They are listed here along with their abbreviations:
- Amplified Bible (Amp)
- Contemporary English Version (CEV)
- King James Version (KJV)
- New Living Translation (NLT)
- The Message Bible (Msg)

At times I have inserted words (in parenthesis) into the Biblical text for clarity. Scripture references appear after the scripture except in Chapters 2 and 3 where I begin most paragraphs with a scripture quotation.

Introduction

Church overseers/bishops representing 160 congregations reported on an exercise to determine the self image of their church. A clear majority scored themselves as healthy congregations. However, only a very small minority were reaching into their communities, seeing lives transformed by Christ. Most were experiencing decadal decline. Half the churches in North America do not lead one person to Christ in a given year."[1] Can a congregation be considered healthy if no adults were baptized or lives transformed in the past five, ten or twenty years?

The church has moved from being central in our culture to being marginal and now is even looked upon as dangerous.[2] One dechurched person said it well, "For many years I have taken to going to church less and less because I find so little there of what I hunger for. It is a sense of the presence of God I hunger for." Of those who attend church regularly, more than half state that the church service is irrelevant to their lives.[3]

A Gallup poll asked, "If you were dying, to whom would you turn for spiritual guidance and comfort?" Only one-third of the adults in the United States said they would turn to a pastor or to a church.[4] Most disheartening of all is that "one in four millennial's (adults ages 18 to 29) have no religious commitment of any kind. Only one percent of college students go to church on Sunday."[5] Some argue that the mega-churches are growing and offset this downward trend. But studies show that eighty percent of their growth is from transfers.[6]

We equate social action and political action with evangelism. We say, "We live a good moral life. That's sufficient." Since when does living a good moral life and serving others get us to heaven? Multitudes from many cultures and religions live a good moral life and have no reverence for Jesus. (John 14:6).

"The gospel says, 'Go,' but our church buildings say 'Stay.' The gospel says, 'Seek the lost,' but our churches say, 'Let the lost seek the church.'"[7] Bill Tenny-Brittian, after consulting with churches for decades, sums it up so well:

> The greatest need of the church is to rediscover and implement two concerns which are the Great Commission and the Great Commandment. They form the central legacy left by our Lord... We've worked with literally hundreds of churches (and observed thousands more), and one truth consistently stands out: The culturally relevant and biblically sound congregations are the most likely to reach the most people with the Gospel.
>
> Unfortunately, many churches begin to lose their passion for these two concerns in as early as the first five years. The average U.S. congregation is riddled with conflict and oppression from a handful of controllers. In addition, congregations worry more about whether or not everyone knows each other than whether or not they carry out the two great concerns of the Lord. Many of the 350,000 churches in the U.S. seldom evidence love for one another and for the stranger.
>
> What pastors hear is, "But pastor, before we go after more new members, shouldn't we take better care of our members?" One only has to look at how most churches spend their money and what most congregations expect of their pastors to know that most churches do not follow our Lord's wishes. No wonder 85 percent of U.S. congregations are either on a plateau or dying.[8]

"We have underestimated the supreme importance of the Church in God's economy. She is the center and motive of all His activity from all eternity. ... She is included as a full partner in all His plans... Jesus is not complete without His Body. ... He has chosen voluntarily to limit Himself in order that the Church may become His judicial equal."[9]

It's the Best Time To Be Alive

The picture becomes much more hopeful when we look at the international Christian community. The Gospel is going around the world at a greater pace than ever before.

According to Global Media Outreach, two million people a day from more than one hundred countries seek for answers to faith questions through this ministry.[10] There are more Muslims coming to Christ in the last fifteen years than in the previous fifteen centuries.

One hundred years ago, one in twenty-one persons identified themselves as Christians; today one in nine professes to be Christian. However, what one claims and how one lives are often miles apart. Some estimate that there are one hundred thousand persons being baptized into the Christian Church every day. According to The Traveling Team, the fastest growing religion in the world is Christianity.[11] World population is increasing by 1.72% annually, while Bible-believing Christians are growing by 6.9% annually. In China alone 30,000 are converted daily, 34,000 in Latin America and 25,000 in Africa. Every fourteen days a new translation of the New Testament is begun in a new language. In the U.S. each year, it takes eighty-five believers to win one to Christ; in Africa and Latin American, it takes four; in Asia and India, it takes one to bring one; and in China, one Christian brings four to Christ each year.

The greatest privilege you will ever have in life is to help someone become a follower and disciple of Jesus. There is nothing more exciting than learning the life story of another person and becoming a part of their story as they become a part of yours.

We are on the winning team. Jesus promised he will build his church. (Matt. 16:18). May the day come soon as John depicts in Revelation 7:9-10: "I looked and there before me was a great multitude that no one could count, from every nation, tribe, people and language, standing before the throne and in front of the Lamb... They cried out in a loud voice: 'Salvation belongs to our God, who sits on the throne, and to the Lamb.'"

Part 1:
Jesus' Mission

1

Jesus' Mission

"The Son of Man came to seek and to save the lost." (Luke 19:10b).

Scores of Scriptures help explain Jesus' mission. Let's begin with perhaps the most familiar one: "For God so loved the world that he gave his one and only Son, that whoever believes in him shall not perish but have eternal life. For God did not send his Son into the world to condemn the world but to save the world through him." (John 3:16-17). Chapter 2 lists forty or more scriptures that underscore Jesus' mission.

The Great Commission

Jesus' Commission is clear: Make disciples of all ethnic groups throughout the world. The standard is not the size of our church building or the number of members, but the extent to which we make fully devoted followers of Jesus who in turn make fully devoted followers of Jesus. If a church is not making disciples can it be called a church?

We are never closer to God than when we are involved with his mission. Jesus was the greatest missionary, and as he was sent, so he sends us. (John 17:18).

His Great Commandments teach us how to fulfill his Great Commission: "You shall love the Lord your God with all your heart and with all your soul and with all your mind" and "You shall love your neighbor as yourself." (Matthew 22:37, 39). If we love God we will love others. Like Jesus we will have a forceful influence on our culture. Since the church has lost much of its influence on our culture, it's appropriate to ask, "Do we love Jesus to the extent that we are making disciples who make disciples?"

Before Jesus went to the cross, He wept over Jerusalem. (Luke 19:14). Jesus' primary emotional response was compassion. He saw people as sheep that had been bruised, beaten, and thrown out. Rather than being filled with contempt, he was filled with love. Too often, those who have been Christians for many years have little compassion for sharing the Good News of the Gospel. Some have sympathy for the lost, but sympathy is weak on action, while compassion cares enough to act. Older churches, as well as older Christians who have walked with Christ for many years, witness less than those who are new in the faith. Thank God there are exceptions. Some mature Christians have great compassion, and some older congregations have not lost their first love. As Micah 6:8 admonishes his people: "Keep all God's salvation stories fresh and present." (Msg).

If you want to understand the compassion of Jesus for lost people, then consider these words in a new context. Imagine you are walking along a path in the twilight enjoying the evening sky, when you hear stifled sounds and muted cries. Your eyes search and see the shadow of a big man. You look closer and see he has a little girl pinned down as he molests her. Jesus sees lost souls this way, harassed and helpless, molested and pinned down by the enemy. If you saw this scene you would be overcome by rage and disgust and be moved to rapid response. No wonder Jesus wept when he saw the crowds as sheep without a shepherd. (Matt. 9:36). When we see a crowd, we need to see the people as Jesus saw them.

Jesus' Mission and the Church

Since the church is the body of Christ, we follow our head who gives us clear instructions with the Great Commandment and the Great Commission.

Jesus gave his life for the church. His mission is intimately related to the church. What is the church? The Greek term is "ekklesia," which means gathering. It has nothing to do with a building. It is not a religious term. It is citizens gathered together for a specific purpose. "It never referred to a specific place, only a specific gathering."[12] Peter's confession in Matthew 16:16 is the church's foundation: the belief that Jesus is the Messiah, the Son of the living God. This was revolutionary. Other religions had imaginary gods. Our God is living!

Neil Cole describes the church as "the presence of Jesus among His people called out as a spiritual family to pursue His mission on this planet."[13] "The church does not exist for us. We are the church, and we exist for the world."[14] God is on a mission and the church is the tool God uses to carry out his mission. Unfortunately, many churches are focused on keeping the reached rather than reaching the lost and making disciples. God can capture our hearts with the irresistible story of Jesus and change the direction of your church's ministry.

Jesus' Commission Is Not a Program but a Lifestyle

It's not enough to have a missions' department. The essence of church *IS* mission. The ethos of the church is mission. This DNA must drive the church. Much of the fatigue we're feeling in the church today is from doing church work, not the work of the church. Our mission is not a program we adopt but a lifestyle.

When I ask what is the purpose of the church, congregations respond that it's to worship God and to build up the people of God. These answers overlook the primary purpose of the church, which is to extend God's reign in our hearts, homes, and communities and finally to the ends of the earth. (Matt. 6:10).

Our Calling

Our calling is to make disciples. As Jesus began his public ministry, he called fishermen Simon and Andrew, "Come after Me and be My disciples, and I will make you to become fishers of men." (Mark 1:17 Amp). Jesus called the disciples to fish for people with the same energy they had used to fish for food. The gospel makes missionaries of all God's people. Being a fisher of men and women is our primary calling. Our personal holiness is important but it is an effect of our salvation, not its cause. Placing our faith in our godly character will not bring us victory. As Oswald Chambers writes, "Paul was not overly interested in his own character. And as long as your eyes are focused on our own personal holiness, we will never even get close to the full reality of redemption. Christian workers fail because they place their desire for their own holiness above their desire to know God... There is no reckless abandon to God in that. God cannot deliver me while my interest is merely in my own character. Paul was not conscious of himself. He was recklessly abandoned, totally surrendered, and separated by God for one purpose – to proclaim the gospel of God."[15]

As the Father Sent Jesus, He Sends Us

In his final words to the disciples, Jesus describes our task, which we call the Great Commission. Jesus said, "All authority in heaven and on earth has been given to me. Therefore go and make disciples of all nations, baptizing them in the name of the Father and of the Son and of the Holy Spirit, and teaching them to obey everything I have commanded you. And surely I am with you always to the very end of the age." (Matt. 28:18-20).

If we begin to comprehend why God sent Jesus, then we will begin to understand our mission and the mission of our church. As the Father sent Jesus, Jesus sends us. (John 17:18; 20:21).

We extend God's Kingdom by giving our allegiance to the Great Commandment and the Great Commission. How we carry out the mandate of the Great Commission is by exercising the Great Commandment. Therefore, we fulfill Jesus' Mission as we are motivated by the Great Commission and function by the Great Commandment.

Every Church "Agrees"

While the vision/mission statement of every church includes the concept of the Great Commandment and the Great Commission, too many Christians and too many churches only give lip service to the Great Commission. Jesus' commands need to become the compelling passion of churches and individuals. Many Christians say they try to live out their faith, but only six percent attempt to share their faith verbally. We agree that service and doing good deeds are essential, but too often our works glorify ourselves rather than bring glory to God. We must intentionally point people to Jesus.

Chapter 2 lists in chronological order a few of the numerous scriptures Jesus uses to describe his mission. In the third chapter we ask, "Did the New Testament authors understand and promote Jesus' mission?" I attempt to "prove" the importance of these two commandments by setting forth these Scriptures in the hope that we will make them the compelling passion of our lives and of the church. Unless this happens, the church will continue to be anemic and eventually die.

Chapters 5, 6 and 7 address three basic pillars every individual and each church needs to implement Jesus' Mission. We must be rooted in God's Word, empowered by the Holy Spirit and energized by prayer.

The remainder of the book demonstrates how we might fulfill the Great Commandment and the Great Commission.

God's Mission Is Evident from the Beginning

From the opening chapters of the Bible, God's mission is to reach the world. "I have raised you up... that I might show you my power and that my name might be proclaimed in all the earth." (Ex. 14:16). God spoke through Moses and the prophets, giving the Old Testament Covenant. We were powerless to keep that Covenant, so God sent Jesus to reach across to us becoming one of us but without sin, so that he could become our high-priest and redeemer. (John 1:14). Jesus moved where we are. Only as we move to where others are and enter their lives as Jesus did can we be effective in God's mission.

Jesus, reading from Isaiah, written seven hundred years before Christ, reminds us that his mission was not an afterthought but originated in eternity. At the beginning of his ministry, he read from Isaiah 61:1-2, "The Spirit of the Lord is on me, because he has anointed me to proclaim good news to the poor. He has sent me to bind the brokenhearted, to proclaim freedom for the captives and release from darkness for the prisoners, to proclaim the year of the Lord's favor and the day of vengeance of our God." (Lk. 4:18-19).

Jesus was willing to be sent and joyfully endured the cross to redeem us. (Heb. 12:2). "I have come down from heaven not to do my will but to do the will of him who sent me." (John 6:38). Jesus' prayer just before his crucifixion was, "Father, if you are willing take this cup from me; yet not my will, but yours be done." (Luke 22:42). It was the will of the Father that Jesus die for the sin of the world. "In him (Christ) we have redemption through his blood, the forgiveness of sins, in accordance with the riches of God's grace that he lavished on us..." (Eph.1:7-8).

Jesus' Passion

Jesus' mission and his passion are one. After twenty years of church consulting work, a church consultant said that for a healthy thriving church, the one common ingredient above all others is spiritual passion.

Floyd McClung writes, "I have discovered that God is more concerned about my passion than my ministry. I have learned that if I keep my heart on fire for him, he will take care of my ministry."[16] Spurgeon said, "A burning heart makes a flaming tongue." Passion grows out of a heart and life of prayer.

Jesus' passion is evident in his teaching. "The crowds were amazed at his teachings, because he taught as one who had authority." (Matt. 7:28-29). He put aside his schedule to heal the sick and explain the Kingdom of Heaven. In nearly every chapter in the Gospels, Jesus reminds us of the urgency and importance to live in obedience to these Great Commandments.

Following Jesus' baptism, Matthew writes, "From that time on Jesus began to preach, 'Repent, for the kingdom of heaven is near.'" (Matt. 4:17). From the beginning of his ministry we see urgency. He calls us to follow him, not in joining him for a life of ease but a life of self-denial.

What Is Preaching?

Jesus said, "I have come to preach." (Mk. 1:35-39). What is preaching? Nearly every time "preach" is used in the Gospels, it refers to presenting the Good News to those who were not his followers. When Jesus spoke to his disciples he was teaching. If we are relating to true followers of Jesus, we are teaching no matter how loud we shout or how high we jump.

Congregations in search of pastoral leadership often say they are searching for a preacher, but if they believe their people are saved, they are searching for a teacher. Followers of Christ need a teacher to equip them to do their ministry in the world. Preaching in the New Testament is a proclamation of salvation and takes place primarily in the marketplace. This misunderstanding is one reason our churches are still on milk rather than meat.

Moving from the Market Place to Church Buildings

When was preaching the Gospel switched from being done in the world to preaching in the secluded confines of a church building? We know that for the first three centuries when the church expanded so extensively, there was not a church building in the Roman Empire. Christians met in homes and perhaps other buildings for study, fellowship, sharing of the bread and for prayer. Then beginning in the fourth century, when Constantine sought to pronounce everyone Christian and persecution ceased, people began to build church buildings. When they did, evangelism and the preaching of the

Gospel to the world basically stopped. Church historian G.J. Herring calls his book on this period, *The Fall of Christianity.* James Rutz in his booklet *Seventeen Hundred Years is Long Enough* writes, "What really killed us was the bricks. In the biggest blunder in our history the church began constructing lots of buildings, displacing the catacombs and the forest glens and ending forever the precious meetings in living rooms."

It's as though this was the devil's plan to silence the Gospel and keep the church from preaching the Gospel in the world. Instead of each Christian sharing the Good News, the church, centuries later, in the missionary movements here and there, began to send out special "missionaries" to preach the Gospel. But the church itself was not missionary. It stayed in the safety of its buildings, developing organization and institutions.

Even as late as the 19th and 20th centuries, some of the greatest preachers in Europe attracted crowds to their cathedrals and tabernacles, while the church was dying.

With the building of churches, people imagine if their group has a great preacher, it has a great church. The "star" is hired to preach the "Gospel" to those who already believe. The church settled down to build bigger and more buildings with fewer people attending. The church became a static establishment. Persons were given titles. A hierarchy developed and entered politics.

Time and again, God sought to switch Christians to the original pattern of preaching the Gospel to the world. Wesley saved England by going into the fields and streets. When the pastors of Ethiopia were in prison and the people were not allowed to congregate in buildings, the church grew by the thousands. China's church is an example of preaching without buildings, and it is growing by millions a year. Study, prayer, and fellowship are done in the homes and shops.

Preachers love the status, seclusion and sanctity within the building and find all kinds of reasons for buildings. Think what different messages preachers would preach if they were preaching in the world. When the work of the church is done inside the four walls, it loses its appeal, luster and effectiveness. Life is divided into the secular and the sacred.[17]

"We will not make the shift from an internal focus to an external focus unless we are willing to change the way we view success. We cannot shift the way we do church without shifting the way we view church."[18]

Paul's Passion

Paul's description of his relationship to Christ describes his passion: "I am the least of the apostles and do not even deserve to be called an apostle, because I persecuted the church of God."(I Cor. 15:9). Five years later in AD 60 he writes, "I am less than the least of all God's people." (Eph. 3:8). Finally near the end of his life he writes, "Jesus Christ came into the world to save sinners, of whom I am the worst." (I Tim. 1:15). Note the progression of thought in Paul's journey with Christ: I am the least of the apostles; next, I am less than the least of all God's people; and lastly, I am the worst of sinners.

The longer Paul walked with Jesus, the more he saw the need for the grace of Christ. One reason we lack zeal and passion for the lost is that we do not see ourselves as needing more grace. If we see ourselves having little need, we receive little grace. If we see ourselves in need of much grace, we receive much grace. Our worst days are never so bad that we are beyond the reach of God's grace, and our best days are never so good that we are beyond the need of God's grace. Paul's passion is expressed in I Cor. 9:22, "I have become all things to all people, so that by all possible means I might save some."

We Have Lost Our Urgency and Passion

For many Christians the Great Commission has become the great omission or simply a suggestion. "A declining interest in mission is a sure sign that a church and its people have left their first love. Nothing is more indicative of the moral decline of the West than Christians who have lost the passion of Christ for a lost world... The real reason millions go to hell without hearing the Gospel... is a theological problem of unbelief. Many churches have slipped so far from biblical teaching that Christians cannot explain why the Lord left us here on earth... Each of the four Gospels gives us a mandate from our Lord Jesus; the mission statement of the Church is the Great Commission... The main activity of the church until Jesus returns... is to go everywhere proclaiming the love of God to a lost world."[19]

For many years I encouraged our small groups to follow the acrostic P-O-W-E-R as a guide for their weekly gatherings. P = prayer, O = open the Word, W = worship, E = encouragement, R = reach out. Most groups do a commendable job with the first four: but it's like hitting a brick wall to get the groups to reach out. We must reignite our passion to proclaim the Good

News. Share the irresistible story of Jesus!

Questions:

1. Do you agree that the longer we are Christians, the less we share Jesus with others? It's the same with churches. Why is this true?
2. Why do we tend to lose our passion for our lost neighbors?
3. Do you agree with the statement that preaching is primarily to those who have never accepted Christ as their Lord, while teaching is for those who are Christians? Do most of our churches need both during the same service?
4. Why do we as believers often resist teaching?
5. Why is it so difficult to get Christians to reach out to others with the Good News of the Gospel?
6. Can sharing the Gospel become a lifestyle for you?
7. Can sharing Jesus become the ethos or compelling passion of your church rather than simply one program among many others?
8. Floyd McClung wrote, "I have discovered that God is more concerned about my passion than my ministry. I have learned that if I keep my heart on fire for him, he will take care of my ministry." Do you agree? See Revelation 3:16.

2

Jesus' Mission Statements in Chronological Order

"From that time on Jesus began to preach, 'Repent, for the kingdom of heaven has come near.'" (Matt. 4:17).

Consider some of the numerous scriptures from the Gospels that speak to the motivation of the Father and his Son Jesus. If we understand Jesus' mission we will understand our mission and hopefully make his mission the priority of our lives and of our church.

We Begin with Jesus' Birth and Conclude with His Death, Resurrection and Ascension

Matt. 1:21 The angel instructed Joseph to name God's Son "Jesus" which means "the Lord saves." Jesus' name points directly to his mission.

Luke 2:49 KJV As a boy, age 12, Jesus had a sense of urgency when he said, "I must be about my Father's business."

John 3:16-17 "For God so loved the world that he gave his one and only Son, that whoever believes in him will not perish but have eternal life. For God did not send his Son into the world to condemn the world but to save the world through him."

The Greek word for "love" is "agape," a self-sacrificing, costly love. It's that same quality of love we are called to give to the Lord, to one another and to the prebeliever as stated in the Great Commandment. (Matt. 22:37-39).

John 4:35 Don't say, "Four months more and then the harvest." The harvest is now. Jesus says that we are to open our eyes and look at the fields! They are ripe for harvest. These Jews were blinded by their prejudice. They went around Samaria, but Jesus had to go through Samaria. (Jn. 4:4). Do we avoid people in our neighborhoods?

Verse 32 also reveals Jesus' passion for people. He told the disciples that he had food to eat that they know nothing about. Winning people to Jesus is more important than our daily bread.

Matthew 4:17 "From that time on Jesus began to preach, ""Repent, for the kingdom of heaven is near.""

Luke 4:18-19 The scroll was handed to Jesus and he read, "The Spirit of the Lord is on me, because he has anointed me to preach good news to the poor. He has sent me to proclaim freedom for the prisoner and recovery of sight for the blind, to release the oppressed, to proclaim the year of the Lord's favor." The year of the Lord's favor is now, the period between Christ's earthly presence and his return for his church.

This Scripture elucidates the broadness of the Good News of Jesus' mission to include deliverance from the cycle of poverty, from exploitation, brokenness, and bondage. It is important to remind people that "Jesus saves." We know he loves and forgives. We must also proclaim the truth that he came to save sinners. We feed the hungry, cloth the naked and provide shelter for the homeless, believing we have fulfilled our assignment. We fail people if we only give them bread but keep silent about the Savior who can meet their true needs, fill their deepest hungers and heal their greatest hurts.

Matthew 4:19, Mark 1:17 Jesus called Peter and Andrew: "Come follow me, and I will *make* you fishers of men." Jesus calls us to follow him. When Jesus calls and we respond, he is going to make something of us. The word "make" means to "form," "mold," "construct" or "create." Our lives are going to influence men and women for eternity. Someone said, "If you are not a fisher of men, I don't know who you are following but you are not following Jesus."

Mark 1:38, Luke 2:43 Jesus healed many people throughout the day and even after sunset. The next morning the crowds returned with their sick, but they could not find Jesus. The disciples found him praying. When they informed Jesus of the needy people waiting, Jesus replied, "Let's go somewhere else to the nearby villages – so I can preach there also. That is why I have come." Jesus turned away from people who needed physical healing in order to preach to those who had never heard the good news of salvation.

Physical healing and driving out demons were not Jesus' primary reason for his coming. He came to announce the Good News. Eyes and hands are important, but Jesus said, if they offend you, gouge them out or cut them off. (Mark 9:43-47).

Matthew 13, Mark 4 In the parable of the sower, we are to be seed sowers or seed scatterers. The seed is God's Word. There is never a shortage of seed. The shortage is seed scatterers. Much of the seed will not bring a harvest but Jesus promises us some seed will bring a harvest. We sow the seed in the field, i.e. in the world. There are weeds, thorns, and many rock-hard hearts, but if we keep spreading God's love we will find good soil and reap a bountiful harvest: 30-, 60- or 100-fold. The church is compromised because many seeds have sprouted and our in our churches but have never rooted and produced a harvest.

Mark 4:26-29 In this parable, seed is scattered on the ground. Night and day, while the farmer is out and about and even while he is sleeping, the seeds sprout and grow. All by itself the soil produces grain. As soon as the grain is mature, he harvests it. Jesus makes the seed grow. We are not responsible for the growth, but we are responsible to scatter the seed.

Mark 5:19-20 When the demon possessed man was healed, he wanted to go with Jesus, but Jesus said, "Go home to your family and tell them how much the Lord has done for you and how he has had mercy on you. The man went away and began to tell in the Decapolis (ten cities) how much Jesus had done for him…"

Matthew 9:36-37 "When Jesus saw the crowds, he had compassion on them, because they were harassed and helpless, like sheep without a shepherd. Then he said to his disciples, 'The harvest is plentiful but the workers are few. Ask the Lord of the harvest therefore, to send out workers into his harvest field.'"

John 6:27 NLT Jesus said, "You shouldn't be so concerned about perishable things like food. Spend your energy seeking the eternal life that I, the Son of Man, can give you. For God the Father has sent me for that very purpose."

Matthew 16:18-19 "You are Peter, and on this rock I will build my church, and the gates of Hades will not overcome it. I will give you the keys of the kingdom of heaven; whatever you bind on earth will be bound in heaven and whatever you loose on earth will be loosed in heaven."

John 8:12 Jesus is the light of the world. Matt. 5:13-16. We are the salt and light in the world.

Matthew 10:34-35 "Do not suppose that I have come to bring peace on the earth. I did not come to bring peace, but a sword. For I have come to turn a man against his father, a daughter against her mother, a daughter-in-law against her mother-in-law – a man's enemies will be the members of his own household." Strife and division caused by allegiance to Jesus are better than no strife and division with no allegiance to Jesus.

The 99 and 1 Principle

Matthew 18:14 Jesus says the owner of one hundred sheep loses one, so he leaves the ninety-nine and looks for the lost one. "In the same way your Father in heaven is not willing that any of these little ones should be lost." In Luke 15:3-7, he says the shepherd searches until he finds the lost sheep. Then he calls his friends and says, "'Rejoice with me: I have found my lost sheep.' I tell you that in the same way there will be more rejoicing in heaven over one sinner who repents than over ninety-nine righteous persons who do not need to repent."

As fully devoted followers of Jesus, we need to leave the flock and search for the lost one. Pastors and church leaders can model this for the larger church body. Get outside the four walls of the church to relate to the lost. Share the irresistible story of Jesus!

John 9:4 Jesus said, "As long as it is day, we must do the work of him who sent me." The "we" includes all who are followers of Jesus.

John 9:39 "For judgment I have come into the world, so that the blind will see and those who see will become blind." Jesus was persistently conscious of judgment, especially the "Last Judgment." Judgment adds urgency to Jesus' mission and to our motivation.

John 10:10 Jesus came to bring life and bring it to the full. John 17:3. Eternal life is to know God and Jesus Christ. This "knowing" is experiential knowledge. It is far more than giving mental assent to some facts about Jesus. He is Lord and he demands our allegiance.

Luke 10:1-24 Jesus selected 72 of his followers and sent them out. No one said, "I can't go. I don't have the gift of evangelism," or "I am not a missionary." All 72 went even though he sent them out as lambs among wolves. They were not to depend on their training, their money or an extra pair of clothes or shoes, but to seek for the person of peace. Seek those who are open to hearing the Good News. In Matthew 10:10, the disciples were to search for the worthy person, the one who indicates signs of interest and acceptance of the Good News.

Luke 13:1-9 What's the purpose of accidents, tragedies or persecution? "There were some… who told Jesus about the Galileans whose blood Pilate had mixed with their sacrifices. Jesus answered, 'Do you think that these Galileans were worse sinners than all the other Galileans because they suffered this way? I tell you, no! But unless you repent, you too will all perish. Or those eighteen who died when the tower of Siloam fell on them – do you think they were more guilty than all the others living in Jerusalem? I tell you, no! But unless you repent, you too will all perish.'" Tragedies occur every day. They should motivate us to turn to God for answers and repent of any sin in our lives.

Luke 13:34 "O Jerusalem, Jerusalem, you who kill the prophets and stone those sent to you, how *often* I have longed to gather your children together as a hen gathers her chicks under her wings, but you were not willing!" Jesus says, "How often I have longed to gather your children." As a follower of Jesus, the ethos of your church and of your life should reflect this passion of our Lord for people who are far from God.

Mark 6:31 So many people were coming and going that they did not have a chance to eat. Jesus said, "Come… and get some rest." The people saw them leaving and ran to where Jesus was going. A large crowd assembled and verse 34 says, "He had compassion on them, because they were like sheep without a shepherd." Jesus set aside his personal desire to get some much needed rest and instead gave his attention to teaching and feeding the 5000. The Greek word for compassion is "splancthna" or a deeper inward feeling. We can also have compassion for people like Jesus.

Luke 14:12-14 "When you give a luncheon or dinner, do not invite your friends, your brothers or relatives, or your rich neighbors. If you do, they may invite you back and so you will be repaid. But when you give a banquet, invite the poor, the crippled, the lame, the blind and you will be blessed. Although they cannot repay you, you will be repaid at the resurrection of the righteous."

Luke 14:15-24 The master sent his servants to invite the guests, but they all made excuses: one just got married, another bought real estate, and yet another purchased farm equipment. The master was angry and told the servants to bring in the poor, the crippled, the blind and the lame but there was still room. The master said, "Go out to the road and country lanes and make them come in, so that my house will be full. I tell you, not one of those men who were invited will get a taste of my banquet."

Luke 15 Jesus used three stories in Luke 15 – the lost sheep, the lost coin and the lost son – to drive home the point that lost people matter to God as much as a lost child would matter to you and me. In fact lost children mean more to him than our lost child means to us. We would do all we could to find our lost child. If we are camping with our two children and they become lost we will search day and night. If we find one child, do we say, "Just forget about the other?" No way! Neither is God willing that any one perish! (II Pet. 3:9). Luke 15 is the only place in Scripture where we are told we can cause a party in heaven.

Matthew 20:1-16 Five different times the landowner went out to hire workers. He asked, "Why aren't you working?" Sometimes people are standing idle because no one has asked them to join this venture called the harvest. The landowner persisted in getting laborers involved until all those willing to work were working.

Mark 10:45 "For even the Son of Man did not come to be served, but to serve, and to give his life as a ransom for many." Jesus said, "If anyone would come after me, he must deny himself and take up his cross daily and follow me." (Lk. 9:23). Not many are called to be martyrs, but Jesus has asked all of us to serve sacrificially to reach those who are far from God.

Luke 19:10 He "came to seek and save that which was lost." Jesus searched for, intentionally looked for lost people who would follow him. God sought Adam and Eve in the Garden; he sought Abraham to move to the Promised Land; he sought Jacob as he fled from Esau; and he is seeking people today.

Luke 19:14 Before Jesus went to the cross, He wept over Jerusalem.

John 12:47 Jesus did not come to judge the world, but to save it.

Matt. 22:1-14 In the parable of the wedding banquet, "The servants went into the streets and gathered all the people they could find, both good and bad and the wedding hall was filled with guests." When we bring the "bad" (the Greek word can be translated wicked persons) to church, we have a messy church. That's whom Jesus said we are to bring.

Matthew 24:14 Jesus said, "The gospel of the kingdom will be preached (announced or proclaimed) in the whole world as a testimony to all nations and then the end will come." Two billion, one hundred million people in our world have never heard the name of Jesus. Fifty thousand die every day who have not heard of Jesus. Evangelism is the battle for the salvation of the world. It continues the ministry of Jesus who came for our salvation.

John 15:16 "You did not choose me, but I chose you and appointed you so that you might go and bear fruit – fruit that will last – and so that whatever you ask in my name the Father will give you."

John 15:27 "You must testify, for you have been with me from the beginning."

John 17 Jesus' prayer reveals his passion. Why did he pray that we be one? So the world would know he was sent from God. (v.12) Why are there so many internal conflicts in churches and in church institutions? The devil knows that if we allow strife, our outreach will be of little effect. Christian unity and harmony are necessities for effective and fruitful witness in extending God's Kingdom. Internal strife robs evangelism.

John 17:18 "As the Father sent me, I am sending you."

John 18:37 When Pilate asked Jesus if he was a king, he replied, "For this reason I was born, and for this I came into the world, to testify to the truth. Everyone on the side of truth listens to me." Romans 2:2 "God's judgment is based on truth." Share this truth.

John 20:21-23 "As the father has sent me, so I am sending you. Receive the Holy Spirit. If you forgive anyone his sins, they are forgiven. If you do not forgive them, they are not forgiven." When people respond to Jesus' invitation, we have the authority and the joy of looking them in the eye and declaring Christ's forgiveness for their offenses and sins. People need to be released from condemnation and judgment. This new freedom enables people to overcome addictive habits. At the same time Jesus said, "If you do not forgive their sins, they are not forgiven." When it is obvious they hate even the sight of you as I have experienced, it is obvious they are rejecting our Lord.

We Are Given Authority

Matthew 28:18-20 Jesus commissions the disciples. "All authority in heaven and on earth has been given to me... Therefore go and make disciples of all nations..." The Great Commission is not a great suggestion. It's a command. Jesus gives us the authority to make disciples. He commands us to teach all that he taught the disciples. We need to be careful not to add to Jesus' commands, or we will become legalistic. This was a major problem in the New Testament and continues to result in many church schisms. Just as important, we are not to water down Jesus' hard sayings, such as loving your enemies, forgiving everyone who hurts you, loving Jesus more than our sons or daughters, or the necessity of denying ourselves and taking up our cross each day.

We Are Given Power

Acts 1:8 We will receive power when the Holy Spirit comes on us enabling us to be witnesses for Jesus, beginning at home and reaching around the earth. Not only are we to be his witnesses, but we are to "witness Jesus." He is already present everywhere. We need to point out to others the evidence of his presence in their lives and in the world around them. We don't bring Jesus to them as much as we are called to make them aware of his presence. This takes the pressure off of us. We work with Jesus rather than for Jesus. Working for Jesus we grow tired, we burn out. Yoke up with him. (Matt. 11:28).

Acts 26:18 After the resurrection and ascension, Jesus sends Paul to the Gentiles to open their eyes and turn them from darkness to light, and from the power of Satan to God, so that they may receive forgiveness of sins and a place among those who are sanctified by faith in Jesus.

Summary – Mission Drives Everything

From the birth of Jesus to his death, we see why he came stated in dozens of scriptures. His motivation was clear. His personal agenda was set aside to fulfill his mission. Everything Jesus did was in response to his mission. Just as Jesus' mission was his passion, it must also be our passion.

The mission and purpose of Jesus included healing the broken-hearted, setting the captives free, and delivering all who are in bondage, emotionally, spiritually, physically and mentally. But the primary mission of our Lord is centered in the cross. His mission is to redeem humanity by bringing them salvation and wholeness both now and for eternity.

My purpose for this chapter was to make clear beyond the shadow of a doubt that Jesus' mission was to extend the reign of God's Kingdom. Therefore if we are convinced that our mission is the same as Jesus', this will change most of the programs of our churches which are internally focused. We will move from a cloister mentality to one of going into all the world to make disciples who make disciples.

We have one main reason to exist: "To make disciples who make disciples."

Questions

1. Which of the many Scripture(s) concerning Jesus' mission speak the most powerfully to you? Explain.
2. Jesus said, as the Father sent him he sends us. (John 17:18; 20:21). Believing these words will have a greater impact than we can imagine.
3. Do you give most of your service time to those inside the church or to those outside the church? Someone said, "The fatigue we experience is from serving ourselves." Do you agree?
4. How does God want you to apply the 99 principle today? Who is the lost sheep you need to rescue? Are there lost sheep in your church?
5. Discuss, "Get people out of the work of the church into church work."

6. Jesus' mission meant everything to him. Is Jesus' mission everything to you? What will it take to wake us up to make Jesus' mission our mission?

7. Jesus' prayer in John 17 reveals his passion. Notice vv. 12, 18 and 20. Verse 20 makes it clear that people are saved "through our message or through our words." Lord help us to live for you but also to speak your message.

3

Jesus' Mission is Upheld by Every New Testament Writer

"All Scripture is God-breathed and is useful for teaching, rebuking, correcting and training in righteousness so that the servant of God may be thoroughly equipped for every good work." (II Tim. 3:16-17).

Did the New Testament authors understand the purpose of Jesus' mission? The following are a few of the many Scriptures from each of the New Testament authors that upheld Jesus' mission.

Paul's Perspective

Romans 9:1-3 Paul writes, "I speak the truth in Christ - I am not lying, my conscience confirms it through the Holy Spirit - I have great sorrow and unceasing anguish in my heart. For I could wish that I myself were cursed and cut off from Christ for the sake of my people..." The Message Bible reads, "I carry with me at all times a huge sorrow. It's an enormous pain deep within me, and I'm never free of it. I'm not exaggerating—Christ and the Holy Spirit are my witnesses..."

How could Paul carry a great sorrow and anguish and at the same time write to the Thessalonians and the Philippians that they are to rejoice always? (I Thess. 5:16, Phil. 4:4). Paul is full of the joy of the Holy Spirit and at the same time, he carries a burden for his people. As followers of Jesus, we must wrestle with this dichotomy on a daily basis.

Romans 1:1 Paul is called to be an apostle or sent one. In verse 5, through Jesus *we*, that's you and me, received grace and apostleship to call everyone.

Romans 1:14-15 "I am obligated both to Greeks and non-Greeks, both to the wise and the foolish. That is why I am so eager to preach the gospel also to you who are at Rome."

I Timothy 1:15 "Here is a trustworthy saying that deserves full acceptance: Jesus Christ came into the world to save sinners, of whom I am the worst."

I Timothy 2:1-4 "This is good, and pleases God our Savior, who wants all men to be saved and to come to a knowledge of the truth."

II Timothy 2:10 "I endure everything for the sake of the elect that they too may obtain the salvation that is in Christ Jesus."

II Timothy 4:5 Paul instructs Timothy to "do the work of an evangelist." Timothy was timid. (II Tim. 1:7). We need to share the Good News even though we are timid and evangelism is not our primary gift.

I Corinthians 9:19-27 "I am a slave to everyone to win as many as possible." Five times in verses 19-23, Paul uses the phrase "to win." He delineates four different groups of people: the weak, the Jews living under the law, the Jews living above or apart from the law, and the Greeks or Gentiles. He used different strategies for each category of persons. He becomes all things to all men so that by all possible means he might save some. (v. 22).

In verses 24-27, Paul uses Olympic imagery to describe his passion. He trains as an Olympian so he can win an eternal crown. He beats his body and makes it his slave to win the prize. That is passion!

I Corinthians 10:33 Paul tries to please everyone in every way so they can be saved.

II Corinthians 4:13 "It is written, 'I believed, therefore I have spoken.' With the same spirit of faith we also believe and therefore speak, because we know that the one who raised the Lord Jesus from the dead will also raise us with Jesus... All this is for your benefit, so that the grace that is reaching more and more people may cause thanksgiving to overflow to the glory of God." Bringing people to Jesus elicits a thanksgiving celebration to God's glory.

II Corinthians 5:10-11 "We must all appear before the judgment seat of Christ, that each one may receive what is due him for the things done while in the body, whether good or bad. Since, then, we know what it is to fear the Lord, we try to persuade men."

II Corinthians 5:18-20 God reconciles us to himself through Christ and then gives us the ministry of reconciliation.

II Corinthians 10:15-17 "Our hope is that, as your faith continues to grow, our area of activity among you will greatly expand, so that we can preach the gospel in the regions beyond you."

II Corinthians 11:23-27 Paul's horrific suffering indicates his passion for spreading the Gospel. "I have been in prison more frequently, been flogged more severely and been exposed to death again and again. Five times I received from the Jews the forty lashes minus one. Three times I was beaten with rods, once I was stoned; three times I was shipwrecked..., I have been in danger from rivers..., from bandits..., from my own countrymen..., from Gentiles, often gone without sleep; I have known hunger and thirst... and I have been cold and naked..."

Acts 17:17 "Every Sabbath he reasoned in the synagogue, trying to persuade Jews and Greeks." (Also Ac. 18:4). Acts 19:8-10. "Paul entered the synagogue and spoke boldly there for three months, arguing persuasively about the kingdom of God... He took his disciples with him and had discussions daily in the lecture hall of Tyrannus. This went on for two years, so that all the Jews and Greeks who lived in Asia heard the word of the Lord."

Acts 20:24 "I consider my life worth nothing to me, if only I may finish the race and complete the task the Lord Jesus has given me, the work of telling others the Good News about God's wonderful kindness and love." Then he adds these words that reveal his passion: "Remember that for three years I never stopped warning each of you night and day with tears." (v. 31)

Philippians 1:4 "I always pray for you... because you have been my partners in spreading the Good News about Christ..." Verses 12-14. "Everything that has happened to me here has helped to spread the Good News; ... and because of my imprisonment, many of the Christians here have gained confidence and become more bold in telling others about Christ." In verses 15-18, he rejoices that the Gospel was preached even from wrong motives.

Philippians 3:18-21 "For, as I have often told you before... with tears, many live as enemies of the cross of Christ. Their destiny is destruction, their god is their stomach, and their glory is in their shame. Their mind is on earthly things. But our citizenship is in heaven. And we eagerly await… the Lord Jesus Christ, who… will transform our lowly bodies…" Notice the words "often" and "tears."

Ephesians 5:16, Colossians 4:5 "Make the most of every opportunity, because the days are evil."

Philemon 6 "I pray that you may be active in sharing your faith, so that you will have a full understanding of everything we have in Christ."

I Thessalonians 2:7-8 "We were gentle among you, like a mother caring for her little children. We loved you so much that we were delighted to share with you not only the gospel of God but our lives as well, because you had become so dear to us."

The Passion of Luke in Acts

Acts is structured around Jesus' commission in Acts 1:8: "You will be my witnesses in Jerusalem, and in all Judea and Samaria, and to the ends of the earth." First they witnessed in Jerusalem to the Jews (1:1 – 6:7), next in Judea and Samaria to the Samaritans (6:8 – 12:24), and finally they took the gospel to the ends of the earth, to the Gentiles (12:25 – 28:31).

Luke was careful to report the spread of the Gospel:

Acts 6:7 "The number of disciples in Jerusalem increased rapidly, and a large number of priests became obedient to the faith."

Acts 9:31 "The church throughout Judea, Galilee and Samaria…was strengthened and grew in numbers…"

Acts 12:24 "The word of the Lord continued to increase and spread."

Acts 16:5 "The churches…grew daily in numbers."

Acts 19:20 "The Word of the Lord spread widely and grew in power."

Acts 28:31 "Boldly and without hindrance Paul preached…and taught about the Lord Jesus Christ."

The Passion of the Author of Hebrews

Hebrews 10:34. "You sympathized with those in prison and joyfully accepted the confiscation of your property, because you knew that you yourselves had better and lasting possessions." Could I joyfully give up every possession or would I, like the rich young ruler, walk away from Jesus? (See Chapter 4, section entitled "Degrees of Judgment" for more on Hebrews.)

The Passion of James

James 5:19-20. "If one of you should wander from the truth and someone should bring him back, remember this: Whoever turns a sinner from the error of his ways will save him from death and cover over a multitude of sins."

The Passion of Peter

Matthew 16:18-19 The church, founded on Peter's confession that Jesus is Lord, is stronger than any opposition Satan and hell can bring against it. What we bind or loose, declare to be lawful or unlawful, is already bound in heaven. We announce what has already been decided by God. We have the privilege of announcing the opening and closing of the Kingdom of God. Peter did that on the day of Pentecost for the Jews in Acts 2, as well as for the Gentiles in Acts 10 and 15.

Acts 4:20 Peter and John were brought before the Sanhedrin because they were teaching the people and proclaiming in Jesus the resurrection of the dead. The authorities had them thrown in prison. When interrogated they said, "We cannot help speaking about what we have seen and heard."

Acts 2:17-20 Peter, on the Day of Pentecost, declared Jesus' mandate to take the Gospel to the ends of the earth. "In the last days, God says, I will pour out my Spirit on all people.... And everyone who calls on the name of the Lord will be saved." But Peter and the apostles didn't translate this message into action. It took persecution to persuade them to share the Gospel. Acts 8:1-4. "On that day a great persecution broke out against the church at Jerusalem, and all except the apostles were scattered through Judea and Samaria... Those who had been scattered preached the word wherever they went."

Acts 10, 11 God let a sheet down from heaven three times to teach Peter to call no man unclean if God accepted him.

I Peter 1:9 "You are a chosen people, a royal priesthood, a holy nation, a people belonging to God that you may declare the praises of him who called you out of darkness into his wonderful light."

I Peter 3:15 "Always be prepared to give an answer to everyone who asks you to give the reason for the hope that you have. But do this with gentleness and respect."

II Peter 3:9-14 "The Lord... is patient with you, not wanting anyone to perish, but everyone to come to repentance. But the day of the Lord will come like a thief. The heavens will disappear with a roar; the elements will be destroyed by fire, and the earth and everything in it will be laid bare. Since everything will be destroyed in this way, what kind of people ought you to be? You ought to live holy and godly lives as you look forward to the day of God and speed its coming."

The Passion of Jude

Jude contends for the purity of the church lest those who claim to be Christians suffer the punishment of eternal fire. (v.7). In verse 23, he writes, "Snatch others from the fire and save them." What a powerful motivation for us to do all we can to save people from the eternal fires of hell. In his short book, Jude gives many examples of those who did not follow God's path and were destroyed.

The Passion of John

John 20:31 "These are written that you may believe that Jesus is the Christ, the Son of God and that by believing you may have life in his name."

John 3:36 "Whoever believes in the Son has eternal life, but whoever rejects the Son will not see life, but God's wrath remains on him." I John 5:12. "Whoever has the Son has life: whoever does not have the Son of God does not have life."

I John 3:16-18 "This is how we know what love is: Jesus Christ laid down his life for us. And we ought to lay down our lives for our brothers. If anyone has material possessions and sees his brother in need but has no pity on him, how can the love of God be in him?" Our neighbor is anyone in need. (Luke 10:30-37).

I John 3:8 "The reason the Son of God appeared was to destroy the devil's work." How did Jesus destroy the devil's work? By expanding the reign of God in the hearts of those around him.

The Churches of Revelation 2 and 3

The churches in Revelation 2 and 3 were established in the fifties and sixties of the first century. Thirty years later John records Jesus' impression of these churches. His clear word for five of the seven churches is "repent."

To Ephesus he says, "You don't love me or each other as you did at first! Look how far you have fallen! Turn back to me and do the works you did at first. If you don't repent, I will come and remove your lamp stand from its place among the churches." (2:4-5, NLT).
To Pergamum, "You have people there who hold to the teaching of Balaam, who taught Balak to entice the Israelites to sin by eating food sacrificed to idols and by committing sexual immorality. Likewise you also have those who hold to the teaching of the Nicolaitans." (2:14-15).

To Thyatira, "You tolerate …Jezebel. By her teaching she misleads my servants into sexual immorality and the eating of food sacrificed to idols… I will cast her on a bed of suffering, and I will make those who commit adultery with her suffer intensely, unless they repent of their ways. I will strike her children dead." (2:20-23).

To Sardis, "You are dead, wake up! Strengthen what remains and is about to die, for I have not found your deeds complete in the sight of my God... If you do not wake up, I will come like a thief, and you will not know at what time I will come to you." (3:1-3).

The church in the United States resembles the church in Laodicea. "I know your deeds, that you are neither cold nor hot. I wish you were either one or the other! So, because you are lukewarm… I am about to spit you out of my mouth. You say, 'I am rich; I have acquired wealth and do not need a thing.' But you do not realize that you are wretched, pitiful, poor, blind and naked. …Those whom I love I rebuke and discipline. So be earnest, and repent. Here I am! I stand at the door and knock. If anyone hears my voice and opens the door, I will come in and eat with him and he with me." (3:15-20).

The book of Revelation describes horrific suffering that should bring people to repentance. But after describing the plagues, John writes, "The rest of mankind that were not killed by these plagues still did not repent of the work of their hands, they did not stop worshiping demons, and idols of gold, silver, bronze, stone, and wood, idols that cannot see or hear or walk. Nor did they repent of their murders, their magic arts, their sexual immorality or their thefts." (9:20-21).

Conclusion

The motivation of every New Testament writer is for God's people to expand the reign of our Lord Jesus. It should be the primary function in our lives and in the life of our church.

Questions

1. Of the many scriptures by all nine of the New Testament writers, which one(s) grip you the most?
2. John uses the term "belief." What does belief mean to you? Is it more than head knowledge or cognitive information? (See Jas. 2:19.)
3. John gives us some insight as to what happens to churches as they age. What is the cure for this? How does a church renew its passion for the lost? (See Rev. 2 and 3.)
4. Peter and John were bold in their witness for Jesus. What caused them to be so fearless? (See Ac. 4:20.)
5. Jude, the Lord's brother, talks about snatching people from the fire. Do you believe Jude's words in light of the dominant theme of God's love as expressed throughout Scripture?
6. Do you realize you are chosen by God? Why did God choose you? (I Pet. 1:9 and John 15:16).

Part 2:
Necessary Pillars to Implement Jesus' Mission

4

Jesus' Mission Must Have a Balanced Theology

"Whoever believes in the Son has eternal life, but whoever rejects the Son will not see life, for God's wrath remains on him." (John 3:36).

God Is Both Loving and Just

I John 4:8; 3:16. "God is love." Love is the primary attribute of God. Most churches preach an unbalanced theology by portraying God as a God of love to the exclusion of God as a God of justice, holiness, righteousness, truth and judgment. The pendulum can swing too far in both directions. Because the dominant characteristic of God as loving is presented in most churches and believed by most Christians, as well as many secular persons, I am focusing on why we must not neglect the subject of God's justice and judgment. Therefore this chapter is purposely a very one-sided picture of God as a God of justice.

The Purpose of God's Love

Before we focus on God's righteousness and justice let's look at why God loves us. From Genesis to Revelation the purpose of God's loving is not only to redeem us but to make us channels of blessing to bring reconciliation to the world. God does love me, so much that he sent his Son to pay for my sin by giving his very life that I might have life. This makes "me" the object of Christianity. If the object of Christianity is me then as David Platt writes:

> When I look for a church, I look for the music that best fits me and the programs that best cater to me and my family. When I make plans for my life and career, it is about what works best for me and my family. When I consider the house I will live; in, the car I

will drive, the clothes I will ware, the way I will live, I will choose according to what is best for me.... This is not Biblical Christianity.

The message of biblical Christianity is not "God loves me, period" as if we were the object of our own faith. The message of biblical Christianity is "God loves me so that I might make him—his ways his salvation, his glory and his greatness—known among all nations." Now God is the object of our faith, and Christianity centers around him. We are not the end of the gospel; God is.

God's reason for loving us is to redeem us but also to use us as instruments to reach all nations. This theme is prominent throughout both the O.T. and N.T. Genesis 12:3b, God says to Abraham, "All the peoples of the earth will be blessed through you." Many centuries later Peter writes: "You are a chosen people, a royal priesthood, a holy nation, God special possession, that you may declare the praises of him who called you out of darkness into his wonderful light."[20]

Justice and Judgment as Motivation for Mission

God is a God of grace and also a God of justice and truth. Jesus was "full of grace and truth." (John 1:14c). "The law was given through Moses, grace and truth came through Jesus Christ." (John 1:17). Grace and truth must go together. One without the other is incomplete. Emphasize grace alone and you have lawlessness. Emphasize truth alone and you can have legalism and bondage.

"Hyper-grace teachers today choose to emphasize only God's love and forgiveness while practically ignoring Jesus' call for His people to walk in wholehearted commitment to the Lord. They preach mostly on forgiveness without repentance and on receiving God's blessing on their circumstances without any conditions. The truth is, it's glorious that we are freely forgiven by Jesus and that He blesses our circumstances; but these truths are in context to seeking to live in a real relationship with Him and in agreement with His leadership and Word."[21]

From the beginning, God's judgment was administered to Adam and Eve for their disobedience. God sent the flood because the people did not repent, even though Noah preached righteousness and repentance for 120 years. God reigned down fire and brimstone on Sodom because of their wickedness. When Jonah preached repentance, they heard his message and repented, and God spared Nineveh. The revival lasted nearly one hundred years, but then Nahum 1:1-6 prophesied concerning Nineveh, "The Lord is a jealous and avenging God; the Lord takes vengeance and is filled with wrath... The Lord will not leave the guilty unpunished... His wrath is poured out like fire."

God's wrath is his righteous and just reaction to our sin. "God is a righteous judge, a God who displays his wrath every day." (Ps. 7:11). Why? Because we sin every day. Habakkuk writes, "Your eyes are too pure to look on evil; you cannot tolerate wrong..." (Habakkuk 1:13). "The arrogant cannot stand in your presence; you hate all who do wrong..." (Psalm 5:5). "Fourteen times in the first fifty Psalms we see similar descriptions of God's hatred toward sinners, his wrath toward liars, and so on."[22]

"We live in a vast cosmos of interconnectedness, and the connections have consequences, and all the consequences come together in God. The Biblical phrase for the coming together of the consequences is judgment day. We can't be reminded too often or too forcefully of this reckoning."[23]

Paul writes, "We make it our goal to please the Lord... For we must all appear before the judgment seat of Christ, so that each of us may receive what is due us for the things done in the body whether good or bad. Since, then, we know what it is to fear the Lord, we try to persuade others. (II Cor. 5:9-11). "Knowing the terror of the Lord, we persuade men..." (v. 11 KJV).

Not only does our fear of God motivate us to share the Good News, his Word is given to keep us from sinning. The children of Israel were fearful of God's voice on Mt. Sinai. "Moses said to the people, 'Do not be afraid, God has come to test you, so that the fear of God will be with you to keep you from sinning.'" (Ex. 20:20). "Evil is avoided by fear of the Lord." (Prov. 16:6 NLT).

William Booth, the founder of the Salvation Army, took a group through an extensive training course lasting several weeks. His final statement may cause us to question his approach, but we see the results of his efforts around the world today. When he finished the course, he said to his apprentices, "I'm sorry our training took so long. If I could take you to hell for five minutes, none of what I've taught you would be necessary."

Justice Is Innate

Does it make sense that Hitler would get off free, while thousands were martyred for Christ? Does it make sense to not hold a serial killer accountable for his actions? Does it make sense to let your obedient child and your disobedient child receive the same rewards? If there were no consequences for our actions, evil would take over the world.

In the time of the judges, everyone did what was right in his own eyes. Life is utter chaos without rules. Why do we have boundaries, referees, umpires, judges? Without them there would be no game.

Why Does the Bible List More Negative Commands than Positive?

God always gives the positive before the negative side. He blesses us with life, with sunshine, rain, clean water, etc. Before God gave the Ten Commandments, he reminds the Israelites that it was his grace that brought them out of slavery in Egypt. After grace, he gave the Ten Commandments. (Ex. 20:2).

God blessed his people, but they chose to go their own way. The long discourses of the prophets are dominated by negatives. Deuteronomy 28 has 54 verses of God's curses and 14 for his blessings. (See also Lev. 26.) Several times, there are more verses given to God's anger and wrath than there are promises of God's love and blessings. In Matthew 23, Jesus' words of condemnation and warning occupy all 39 verses.

The closer Peter and Paul came to the end of their lives, the more they emphasized sound doctrine and warning against false teachers. They rebuked more than they encouraged. Why? Because it is an inherent part of our old nature to go astray. They rebuked and corrected from a heart of love. In Romans 2:4, the goodness of God is meant to lead us to repentance. Adam and Eve were surrounded by every good thing, but they chose the one forbidden fruit.

We tell our children that we trust them to make the right decisions. If they make wrong decisions, they suffer the consequences. We need to share what the consequences will be. It's the same with our relationship with God. So why do we neglect to proclaim the consequences? Are we afraid people won't like us? Are we afraid people will not return to church?

The Devil's Greatest Weapon

The devil's greatest weapon is causing Christians to question his existence and the reality of judgment. We can't imagine our good neighbors who volunteer as ambulance drivers, fire fighters or school teachers going to eternal darkness, separated from God who is light. (Ro. 1:20-21, 32; Ps. 19:1-4; Jn. 1:9).

Perhaps the primary torment of hell is the regret of remembering they saw God in every kind act, in the birth of a child and in the beautiful views of God's creation, but they shut their minds and eyes to it.

"If we knew the horrors of the potential judgment that hangs over us—if we really believed in what is coming—how differently we would live. Why aren't Christians living in obedience to God? Because of their unbelief... No one should go to hell today without hearing about the Lord Jesus. To me this is an atrocity much worse than the death camps of Hitler's Germany or Stalin's Russia. As horrible as the 1.3 million abortions are in the United States each year, the eternal loss of multiplied millions of additional souls every year is the greatest preventable tragedy of our times."[24]

Why Was the Old Testament Written?

Why was the Old Testament written? In I Corinthians 10:6-10, Paul gives accounts when God punished Israel for their disobedience. In one day 23,000 were killed. Then he writes, "Now these things occurred as examples to keep us from setting our hearts on evil things as they did." Jude 5-7 lists several illustrations of God's judgment in the Old Testament and then concludes, "They serve as an example of those who suffer the punishment of eternal fire."

Is God's Judgment Just?

"True and just are his judgments." (Rev. 19:2). "Shall not the Judge of all the earth do right?" (Gen. 18:25). He will do right even though those who have never heard will, according to our knowledge, be lost. John 14:6 and Acts 4:12 make it clear that there is no salvation in any other name. He will make a righteous judgment. God will judge his people with equity. (Ps. 96:10, 13; 7:11; 9:8). Other translations say, "God will judge his people with fairness or in righteousness."

Our responsibility is to invite people to Jesus who rescues us from the coming wrath, so they receive God's eternal life! (I Thess. 1:10). God's wrath is not uncontrolled anger. He is just and righteous in all his punishment for our rejection of his sacrificial love. Our Lord does not "send" anyone to hell. We choose to go there when we close our hearts to all that he has done to bring us to heaven.

Joe, the golfer, invited Sam to go golfing Sunday morning. Sam said, "Sunday, I'm in church." Joe said, "Give up that nonsense. You know you don't believe it." Sam replied, "What do you mean?" "I can prove you don't believe," replied Joe. "I worked with you every day for twenty years. The Bible says that I'm headed for hell, but you were never concerned enough to urge me to consider changing my life." Ask yourself, "Am I like Sam?"

Ted Haggard writes, "Every morning our church receptionist places a copy of the obituaries from the morning paper on every church staff member's desk. Attached is a post-it note that says, 'Today from Colorado Springs people will go to heaven and people will go to hell. The percentage of people going to heaven and the percentage of people going to hell today is determined by how well you did your job yesterday. If you remember heaven today, it will help someone else avoid hell tomorrow.'"[25]

Culture

Jim Denison writes on Denison Forum, "We are so committed to tolerance that we are rejecting the One who cannot tolerate our sin."[26] Our culture teaches us that there are no absolutes and no sin. If there is no sin there is no guilt; so naturally there can't be any punishment for sin, since there is no sin. Jesus taught more about hell and eternal punishment than any New Testament writer. "Whoever believes in the Son has eternal life, but whoever rejects the Son will not see life, for God's wrath remains on him." (Jn. 3:36). To the religious leaders Jesus said, "How will you escape being condemned to Hell?" (Matt. 23:33).

In Matthew 5 and 6, Jesus repeatedly sets forth the consequences of our sin. If we lose our saltiness, we will be thrown out and trampled by men. Unless our righteousness is superior to the Pharisees, we will not enter the kingdom of heaven. Anyone who says, "You fool!" will be in danger of the fire of hell. If your hand or your eyes offend you, remove them, because it is better to lose them than for you to be cast into hell. If we don't forgive others, the Father will not forgive us. The frequency of these judgment references, some of which are lengthy, remind us of their importance.

Degrees of Judgment

God does everything well and exercises justice. Several scriptures make it clear that there are different degrees of punishment. (Luke 10:12-15). Those who reject the Gospel will be punished more than those in the wicked cites of Sodom, Gomorrah, Tyre, and Sidon. (Luke 12:47-28). Those who know what their master wants, but do not do it, will be beaten with many blows, but the one who does not know will be beaten with few blows. (Mark 12:40, Luke 20:47). Teachers will be judged more severely. (James 3:1).The religious leaders will be punished severely because they mistreated the widows and the poor.

In Matthew 5:19, Jesus said, "Anyone who sets aside one of the least of these commands and teaches others accordingly will be called least in the kingdom of heaven, but whoever practices and teaches these commands will be called great in the kingdom of heaven."

"For if the message spoken by angels was binding, and every violation and disobedience received its just punishment, how shall we escape if we ignore such a great salvation?" (Heb. 2:2-3). If disobedience to the law brought punishment, disobedience to God's greater salvation in the New Testament will bring even greater punishment. See also Hebrews 10:26-30.

"See that no one is sexually immoral, or is godless like Esau, who… sold his inheritance rights… Afterwards, … when he wanted to inherit this blessing, he was rejected. He could bring about no change of mind, though he sought the blessing with tears… You have come to God, the judge of all men... to Jesus the mediator of a new covenant, and to the sprinkled blood that speaks a better word than the blood of Abel… If they did not escape when they refused him who warned them on earth, how much less will we, if we turn away from him who warns us from heaven?" (Heb. 12:14-15).

Frequency of Judgment References

God's wrath and anger are mentioned nearly 500 times in the Scriptures with 53 occurrences in the New Testament. In I Thessalonians 1:9-10, Jesus rescues us from the coming wrath. In I Thessalonians 2:16, the wrath of God has come on the Jews who killed Jesus and the prophets. In Colossians 3:6, the wrath of God is coming on all who practice greed, sexual immorality, anger, rage, filthy language, etc.

The majority of Jesus' fifty-some parables refer to judgment. Many conclude with words such as, "they will be thrown into the fiery furnace, where there will be weeping and gnashing of teeth," a phrase used by Matthew six times. (Matt. 25:30). If we bury our talents, we will be thrown into outer darkness.

"Thirteen percent of Jesus' teaching is about the coming judgment of God... The primary attribute of God is not love but holiness."[27] Without holiness, we will not see the Lord. (Heb. 12:14).

"The Bible refers to hell 167 times... John describes the place of final and eternal punishment as the 'lake of fire' (Rev. 20:15). God did not establish hell for the purpose of scaring people into heaven. Nevertheless, it is a biblical fact that a place of eternal punishment exists, and those who do not know Jesus as their Savior ignore it to their own destruction."[28]

We know John 3:16: "God so loved the world that he gave his one and only Son that whoever believes in him shall not perish but have eternal life." However, the same chapter also gives us verse 36, "Whoever believes in the Son has eternal life, but whoever rejects the Son will not see life, for God's wrath remains on them."

"Our God is a consuming fire." (Heb. 12:29).

God's Creation as Motivation for Mission

Creation has design and purpose. Why would God go to all the effort to create the world and the universe, if he didn't have a plan? "The earth is the Lord's and everything in it, the world and all who live in it." (Ps. 24:1). The whole creation has been groaning as in the pains of childbirth. (Ro. 8:22). His creation is so important that he will redeem it. Even the new heaven and the new earth are pictured in terms of our earthly creation: a river from God's throne, fruit trees that bear fruit all year. (Rev. 22:1-3).

Science has become America's God, producing millions of agnostics and atheists. Scientists can't explain existence. Science has influenced and spoofed many Christians into thinking it was atheistic evolution that brought the world into being. Even many who believe God as their creator are often tightlipped, because it is not politically correct to say so. The Bible refers to God's creation thousands of times. Hundreds of times the Bible declares that God is the creator. "The heavens declare the glory of God…" (Ps. 19:1-3; see also Ps. 50:6; 89:5-8; 97:6; 148.)

In Romans 1:18-25, Paul reminds us of God's obvious stamp-print on all his creation: "The wrath of God is being revealed from heaven against all the godlessness and wickedness of men who suppress the truth by their wickedness, since what may be known about God is plain to them, because God has made it plain to them. For since the creation of the world God's invisible qualities—his eternal power and divine nature—have been clearly seen, being understood from what has been made, *so that men are without excuse.* For although they knew God, they neither glorified him as God nor gave thanks to him, but their thinking became futile and their foolish hearts were darkened…Therefore God gave them over to the sinful desires of their hearts, to sexual impurity for the degrading of their bodies with one another. They exchanged the truth of God for a lie…"

God made every snowflake different, every blade of grass exudes life, and every flower shouts the beauty of God. Every raindrop indicates his love and mercy as it replenishes the earth. Every newborn baby illustrates his creativity. All seven billion of us have different finger prints. Who can believe that a computer or a watch just happened? They were planned by a designer. If you drop Scrabble letters a zillion times over a million years, will you come up with a page of writing that makes sense?

Martin Luther said, "Our Lord has written the promise of the resurrection not in books alone, but in every leaf in spring-time." God's intricate design shouts purpose all around us. Learn to recognize his marvelous creation and declare his praises to all generations.

The Atonement as Motivation

We can't imagine the sacrifice our Heavenly Father made by giving his only Son, or the sacrifice his Son made in leaving heaven and coming to redeem us. All this is beyond our comprehension. Jesus was born of a poor peasant virgin, raised in a poor family, rejected and misunderstood by his own family and relatives. The passion of our Lord reaches its zenith on Good Friday. "God made him who had no sin to be sin for us, so that in him we might become the righteousness of God." (II Cor. 5:21). The cross expresses the magnitude of His love for us. His suffering was a by-product of his passion. While the physical torture was indescribable, the suffering of Christ to pay for our sins is beyond our wildest imagination. What tremendous love! Peter says, "We are not redeemed with gold or silver but with the precious blood of Christ." (I Pet. 1:18-19).

Why would Jesus take our sin upon himself if salvation was not important? He loves us and wants to be with us for eternity. (Jn. 14:2). "The Lord's not slow in keeping his promise… he is patient with you, not wanting anyone to perish, but everyone to come to repentance." (II Pet. 3:8). Such love demands our total devotion.

The Witness of the Martyrs Indicates Passion

The church is a miracle. Throughout history, emperors and rulers have tried to stamp it out. Today in some countries, church buildings are burned and Christians die for their faith, and yet the church survives and often thrives. The New Testament had few if any buildings, programs, clergy, budgets or charismatic personalities, and yet it flourished. Tertullian said, "The blood of the martyrs is the seed of the church."

A clear indicator of the urgency to share the Good News is the witness of Christian martyrs. Why would someone die for Christ? All the apostles were martyred except John, and he was banished and suffered on the Isle of Patmos till he died. When Jesus was betrayed by Judas and taken by the Roman soldiers, the disciples all forsook him and fled. They hid behind locked doors in fear of the Jews. But within a matter of a few weeks, that all changed. They became bold witnesses for Christ. "They did not love their lives so much as to shrink from death." (Rev. 12:11).

Gordon-Conwell Seminary reports that each year there are 171,000 persons martyred for their faith. Why would millions of people be tortured to death for the cause of Christ? They took Jesus' commission seriously.

Roman Catholic Cardinal Francis George said, "I expect to die in bed, my successor will die in prison and his successor will die a martyr in the public square. His successor will pick up the shards of a ruined society and slowly help rebuild civilization, as the church has done so often in human history."[29]

In Revelation 12:11, John writes that the believers overcame Satan by the blood of the lamb and the word of their testimony.

Our mission must capture us. If we don't live with a passionate mission, we live a mediocre life that attracts no one to the Gospel. God calls you and me to be about our Father's business. Frank Laubach wrote, "We are Christlike just in proportion as we possess that passion for souls." We don't have Jesus unless we give him away.

Rewards as Motivation

Those who lead many to righteousness will shine like stars forever and ever. (Dan. 12:3).

Paul writes that he has become all things to all men to win them to Christ so that he can share in its blessings. (I Cor.9:22-23).

Eight successive times in Matthew 5:3-12, Jesus says we will receive a blessing: if we are poor in spirit, if we mourn, if we become meek, if we long for righteousness and justice, if we show mercy, if we walk in purity, and if we become peacemakers. He tells us we will be persecuted, but we are to rejoice because we have a great reward in heaven. If we keep his commandments, we also have a great reward. (Matt. 5:19). We are given eternal rewards as we give to those in need, and as we pray and fast, not to be seen by others, but to please him. (Matt. 6:1-18).

In Matthew 10:40-42, Jesus reminds us that if we give a cup of cold water in His name and entertain a prophet or a righteous person, we will be rewarded.

If we humble ourselves like a child, we will be greatest in the Kingdom of Heaven. (Matt. 18:4). In the parable of the King's servants, one is given ten talents, another five and another one. Those who put their money to work were rewarded with ten cities or five cities according to their ability.

Five different crowns are mentioned in the New Testament: (1) the crown of life for all who persevere in trial (Jas. 1:12, Rev. 2:10); (2) a crown of righteousness (II Tim. 4:8); (3) a crown of glory (I Peter 5:4); (4) a crown of rejoicing (I Thess. 2:19); and (5) an eternal crown (I Cor. 9:25). We are co-heirs with Christ. (Ro. 8:17). Can there be a greater motivation?

Questions

1. How often do you thank the Lord for his suffering and death? Is there a relationship between the consciousness of his sacrifice for us and our faithfulness in witnessing to others?

2. Do you agree with David Platt that the message of biblical Christianity is "God loves me so that I might make him—his ways and his salvation, his glory and his greatness—known among all nations." Are you conscious every day of God using you to make him known?

3. It is not politically correct to talk about the justice or the judgment of God. Jesus often used parables. What parables/stories can you use to present the truth that God is both just and one who demands faith, righteousness and holiness? (Heb. 11:6; 12:14).

4. Do you agree that the devil's greatest weapon is causing Christians to question his existence and the reality of judgment?

5. Are you conscious of the thousands who are persecuted or martyred for Christ each year? Do you pray for a consciousness of the call to suffer and the call to witness?

6. Rewards are mentioned frequently in the Bible. Hebrews 11:6. "Without faith it is impossible to please God, because anyone who comes to him must believe that he exists and that he rewards those who earnestly seek him." When you lose your zeal for the Lord, do you remember the rewards he promised you? Do the promised New Testament rewards help you live zealously for the Lord? Why or why not?

Chapters 5, 6 and 7 address three basic pillars every individual and church needs to implement Jesus' Mission. We must be rooted in God's Word, empowered by the Holy Spirit and energized by prayer.

5

Jesus' Mission is Undergirded by the Bible

God's Word is truth. (John 17:17).

The secular mind with its "enlightened" scientific worldview cannot tolerate absolutes. Our culture makes one exception when it comes to absolutes, only one: "There are no absolutes," which of course, is an absolute. Bible-believing evangelical Christians base their faith on the absolutes found in Scripture.

The Scriptures were read each Sabbath in the synagogue. Jesus likely memorized the complete Torah. Today, Orthodox Jews lock the Torah in a secure cabinet to preserve and set it apart from all other books. I feel confident Jesus also memorized such Scriptures as the following:
- "My soul is consumed with longing for your laws at all times." (Ps. 119:20).
- "Oh, how I love your law! I meditate on it all day long." (Ps. 119:97).
- "Your word is a lamp to my feet and a light for my path." (Ps. 119:105).
- "I have treasured the words of his mouth more than my daily bread." (Job 23:12b).

When Jesus was tempted, he said repeatedly, "It is written." When he was challenged by the Pharisees, Sadducees, the Greeks or Romans, Jesus frequently quoted the Old Testament Scriptures.

Jesus and the Word are so closely identified that he says, "If you remain in me and *my words* remain in you, ask whatever you wish, and it will be given you." (Jn. 15:7).

Dr. Luke introduces the church in Acts 2: "They devoted themselves to the

Apostle's doctrine..." "The phrase means that they persisted in listening to the apostles as they taught. ... We should count it a wasted day when we do not learn something new and when we have not penetrated more deeply into the wisdom and grace of God."[30] Peter and Paul remind us to grow in the knowledge of God. (I Pet. 3:18, II Tim. 2:15).

Bible Schools and Seminaries

Today, many seminaries teach psychology, philosophy, and business principles, often at the expense of the Scriptures. They teach "management" and "how to keep the peace," but are weak on Biblical vision. Vision grows out of a vibrant faith that is grounded in the Scriptures. Some seminaries label much of the Old Testament that I believe is historical accounts as simply allegory. This tends to put a shadow over the text and opens the door wider than necessary for the human interpretation, which robs the text of its authority.

Memorization Need Not Intimidate You

When Jesus and the New Testament writers quoted the Old Testament, they often gave the essence. I have found memorizing word for word can easily become a legalistic and frustrating exercise especially with so many different versions.

When sincere Christians quote Scripture from memory with expression and authority, the Holy Spirit takes these words to the hearts of the people. In Acts 2:37, the people were cut to the heart as Peter spoke quoting many Old Testament Scriptures. The Word was also backed up with ten days of prayer and with the power of the Holy Spirit. Too often we have a form of godliness but no power or authority, because God's words are not undergirded with prayer and the Holy Spirit's anointing. (II Tim. 3:5). Paul writes, "Let the word of Christ dwell in you richly (let it have the run of the house) as you teach and admonish one another with all wisdom, and as you sing psalms, hymns and spiritual songs with gratitude in your hearts to God." (Col. 3:16).

Overcoming Temptation

It's not enough to "magically" quote Scripture to overcome temptation. Jesus was anointed by the Holy Spirit just before his temptation, when he answered the Devil with Scripture. (Lk. 3:21-22). To be effective, the

Scriptures need to be accompanied with the Holy Spirit's anointing.

The Word Must Shape Us

If we dwell in the Word, that is let the Word speak to us in our situation, it will transform us. As we learn to live within God's Word, we find Scripture begins to "read" us rather than we read the Scriptures. That takes time. The average American watches television 34 hours a week and spends 10 or more hours on the internet. Apparently the television and the internet are more important than God's Word! Don't say you don't have time to read and study God's Word! You have time for what is important. The answers to our anemic churches are not found in our programs, methods and strategies, but in God's Word and in being led by his Spirit.

The Scriptures must be our main diet. Other Christian authors are helpful; however, all authors have a skewed theology which is impacted by their personality, their experiences and their cultural context. Reading several authors and studying with other mature believers will go a long way toward correcting this weakness. Some study a particular author and end up quoting him or her more than the Scriptures, which can lead to teaching that is more human-centered than Christ-centered and can eventually become false doctrine. No author, no matter how godly, will trump the Scripture.

Brad Lomerick writes the following:

> Too many build up their heads without minding their hearts. They read books and attend conferences, but spiritual development is often ignored. According to our research, only eleven percent of Christian leaders say passion for God is the leadership trait that best describes them....Passion for God makes us generous, active and bold. If you're struggling to become a better leader, perhaps you should put down that sales book or take a break from those online videos on time management. Instead nurture your spiritual development first. Petition God to light a fire for His glory inside of you. Spend time in prayer and reflection and in the Scriptures. Develop your heart for God and trust that He will help you lead well.[31]

My friend Brian, a truck driver, hands out hundreds of New Testaments. Many tell him they don't have time to read. Brian says, "I don't have time either." They respond, "What do you mean you don't have time, you're always quoting Scripture." Brian carries a New Testament in his pocket. He has several in his truck. Testaments can be found all over the house especially in the bathroom. They are marked up and bent out of shape. You can tell Brian loves the Word.

The Word Shapes Our World View

Most American Christian families listen to the television all evening, go to bed, breath a prayer, get up and have a five minute devotional time. They wonder why their lives are not full of the fruit of the Spirit and often have to fight feelings of depression. Five minutes a day will not offset a couple hours of television each evening. Saturday night television will not help you digest the pastor's message on Sunday.

The world-view of most Christians comes from the news commentators rather than the Bible. We all have a choice on what shapes our world view - we can feed our minds on what the news commentators tell us each night on TV, or we can dive into God's Word to shape our character and guide our values.

A Verse a Day?

"Many Western Christians have been deluded into thinking that a verse a day keeps the devil away. For many, their entire intake of God's Word consists of reading a daily verse off a calendar and listening to a Biblical sermon once a week. Unfortunately, this shallowness leads to a weak faith and a lack of fruit for the Kingdom of God. Jesus' parables describe abundant sowing of the seed, seemingly indiscriminate of where it lands. To see the life of the Kingdom germinate, grow and bear fruit, God's Word must be received abundantly and it must penetrate deeply into our souls. If you do not plant the seed, you will not grow the life and see the fruit. It is that simple."[32]

Read and reread large portions of Scripture until you know what is in each chapter of a book. For the Gospel begin with Mark or John. For the N.T. letter read Philippians every morning for a week and you will begin to feel familiar with the text. It will start to become a vital part of your thought life. If you read five Psalms a day and one chapter of Proverbs for a month you will have read those books through. Your life will be changed.

Understand the Setting

One of the helpful and important aspects of studying and understanding the Scripture is to understand the setting. The Life Application Bible (Zondervan) introduces each book with the purpose, author, original audience, date written, setting, key verses, key people and key places. Too often we read a Scripture with no understanding of its original purpose and context; then we wonder why it is not making sense with other Scriptures, or why it does not seem relevant to our situation.

At Brook Hills Church in Birmingham, Alabama, they decided to take away music, screens and air conditioning, and see if the people would come on Friday evenings to study the Word. They call it Secret Church. It begins at six p.m. and goes to midnight. They interrupt the six-hour Bible study periodically to pray for brothers and sisters around the world who are forced to gather secretly. They also pray for themselves, that they learn to love the Word as those who gather in secret. Amazingly they have to take reservations because they cannot contain all the people who want to come. They never end on time.[33]

Interpreting the Word

The early church interpreted the Word in the context of community as groups met in homes. "The Bereans were of more noble character than those in Thessalonica, for they received the message with great eagerness and examined the Scriptures every day to see if what Paul said was true." (Acts 17:11). Can you imagine what would happen if we would meet together every day to examine the Scriptures? Most small groups or cell groups find it very difficult to meet weekly.

The early Christians devoted themselves to the Scriptures every day to be taught. (Acts 2:41, 46-47). The author of Hebrews admonishes us, "Consider how we may spur one another on toward love and good deeds, not giving up meeting together as some are in the habit of doing, but encouraging one another..." (Heb.10:24-25).

Scripture and Leadership Teams

Leadership meetings are usually taken up with agenda items that deal with internal challenges and problems. There is often very little time given to prayer or the study of Scripture. If your leadership team would begin with a study of Scripture and earnest prayer, perhaps taking 45 minutes or an hour, you will find God-given insight for the items on the agenda that you didn't know was possible. The supernatural will be there, and your faith will grow. God will enable you to move the congregation to a new level.

Our American mind-set is to get prayer out of the way, so we can get on with the real work. Until that changes, we will not be producing disciples who make disciples.

The Place of Preaching

The early church gathered in homes and in larger groups to hear the reading and explanation of the Word. "Preaching is a spiritual gift God gives to certain leaders so they can minister the Word in power to sizable groups of people. Without the preaching of the Word, smaller groups tend to drift off and fizzle. They need to see themselves as a part of something larger. When leaders stand before the church and declare the Word with passion and spiritual conviction, the whole church tends to unify around the great truths of God.... They gain vision."[34] Paul taught the Ephesians publicly, in large meetings, and in small groups that met in their homes. (Ac. 20:20).

Paul instructs Timothy to be diligent to study the Word, so he can interpret it accurately. (II Tim. 2:15). He reminds the Romans, "Everything that was written in the past was written to teach us, so that through endurance and the encouragement of the Scriptures we might have hope." (Ro.15:4).

Paul couldn't have been more forceful as he writes to Timothy, "I solemnly charge you in the presence of God and of Christ Jesus, who is to judge the living and the dead...preach the Word; be prepared in season and out of season; correct, rebuke and encourage – with great patience and careful instruction." (II Tim. 4:1-2a). Paul knew that unless the Word is preached with power, false teachers would creep in and penetrate the church.

Paul is compelled to preach. "I am compelled to preach. Woe to me if I do not preach the gospel!" (I Cor. 9:16). Perhaps Paul learned from Jeremiah, who wrote that God's Word is like a fire shut up in his bones. He cannot hold it in. (Jer. 20:9). Martin Lloyd-Jones describes preaching as "Theology coming through a man who is on fire."

Today, many pastors and teachers stand before their congregations and feed them good psychological truths or techniques, but do not deal with the root problem of sin. This may help, but it will not bring transformation to the human self-centered nature that is in each one of us. It is through the Word of God, empowered by the Holy Spirit, that we are born into a living hope. Because we have this hope, we purify ourselves just as he is pure. (I John 3:3). James reminds us that it's the Word planted within us that gives us our daily salvation. (1:21).

It's the truth that sets us free! (John 1:25; 8:36). "God's Word is truth." (John.17:17b). False teachers will deny the truth, "abandon the faith and follow deceiving spirits and things taught by demons. Such teachings come through hypocritical liars, whose consciences have been seared as with a hot iron." (I Tim. 4:1-2).

Sharing the Good News Motivates Growth in Our Understanding of Scripture

When people love the Word, they'll love to share it with others. "I pray that you may be active in sharing your faith so that you will have a full understanding of every good thing we have in Christ." (Phm. 6). When we share what we learn, it becomes deeply rooted in our lives, and we grow in our understanding of Christ. When we share the Good News, we are motivated to study so we can explain it to those we are mentoring and discipling. Of course the reverse is true: if we are not sharing the Word of God, we will not have the motivation to study it. Furthermore, if we only study alone, we are prone to be influenced by our personality, our temperament and our context. Studying with other sincere followers of Jesus will help to give us a balanced theology, and a greater boldness to speak with confidence and power.

Passion Is Related to Our Self-Image

As we saturate ourselves in God's Word, our passion grows out of discovering who Jesus says we are in Christ. Jesus said that John the Baptist was greater than all the Old Testament prophets, and that we are greater than John. (Matt. 11:11). John was greater than the Old Testament prophets because he had the wonderful privilege of introducing the Messiah, whom he baptized, while the Old Testament prophets only longed to see this day. Even the angels longed to see this day. (Lk. 10:23-24, I Pet. 1:10-12).

How is it possible for Christians today to be greater than John the

Baptist? It's all because of the resurrection and Pentecost. The Word says approximately 200 times that Jesus is in me and I am in him. With Jesus in me, I can do more things than I can imagine. (Phil. 4:13, Eph. 3:20-21). Paul reminds us that we are seated with Christ far above all the rulers and authorities, and above every problem we might face. (Eph. 1:20-23; 2:6). Believing these Scriptures cannot coexist with a poor self-image. These truths empower us with zeal and passion.

The Word of God Is Powerful

"The word of God is living and active. Sharper than any double-edged sword, it penetrates even to dividing soul and spirit, joints and marrow; it judges the thoughts and attitudes of the heart." (Heb. 4:12).

All Scripture is inspired, (II Tim. 3:16-17), but some Scriptures are not as applicable for today as others. For example we do not stone our son if he is rebellious. (Deut. 21:18-21). If we have a skin rash we don't go to the priest. (Lev. 13). Six times in the New Testament, we are told to greet one another with a holy kiss. In our context we need to apply the principle behind this admonition, which is to show genuine affection for our brothers and sisters in Christ.

The Word of God Is Understandable

Everyone can understand Jesus—everyone who wants to... When Jesus told a story about a father's broken heart everyone understood. When, dying on the cross, he asked God to pardon his enemies, no one needed a dictionary or a commentary to know what he meant. Whether one is a Jew of the 1st Century or a Chinese of the 20th Century, whether he lives in the country or the city, whether he is rich or poor, learned or ignorant, a success or failure, he can understand Jesus, for Jesus is translatable into every tongue. Time and place do not count. The Sermon on the Mount is not worn by the passing of time, nor is the light of the Transfiguration dimmed by 10,000 miles of space. Jesus is, so to speak, in heaven and, like the stars, he shines as brightly in the southern skies as he does over the North Pole.[35]

We Interpret Scripture Through the Lens of Jesus Christ

While all Scripture is inspired by God, it's important to interpret the Word through the lens of Jesus Christ. "In the past God spoke to our forefathers through the prophets... but in these last days he has spoken to us by his Son, whom he appointed heir of all things, and through whom he made the universe. The Son is the radiance of God's glory and the exact representation of his being..." (Heb. 1:1-3). Jesus did not come to abolish the Old Testament law but to fulfill it. (Matt. 5:17). Six times in Matthew 5, Jesus said, "You have heard it said, but I say to you." Then he contrasts murder with anger, adultery with lust, divorce with faithfulness, vows with honesty, revenge with kindness, and hate with love for the enemy. Christ is the end of the law, so that there may be righteousness for everyone who believes. (Romans 10:4).

The Scriptures point to Jesus. "Beginning with Moses and all the Prophets, he explained to them what was said in all the Scriptures concerning himself." (Lk. 24:17). "The Law and the Prophets were proclaimed until John. Since that time the Good News... is being preached..." (Lk. 16:16). "You diligently study the Scriptures because you think that by them you possess eternal life. These are the Scriptures that testify about me..." (Jn. 5:39). "In the past God overlooked such ignorance, but now he commands all people everywhere to repent." (Ac. 17:30, Ro. 3:25).

Jesus is the living Word. (Jn. 1:1). The church is the "pillar and foundation of the truth." (I Tim. 3:15). Timothy was to guard the truth that was entrusted to him. (II Tim. 1:14). The best way to guard the truth is to know, obey and propagate it so profusely that the enemy can't silence it.

Concerning the Old Testament, Paul writes, "These things happened to them as examples and were written down as warnings for us on whom the fulfillment of the ages has come." (I Cor. 10:11). Again, "These things occurred as examples to keep us from setting our hearts on evil things as they did." (I Cor. 10:6).

Jesus is the supreme revelation of God. We interpret the Scriptures through the lens of Jesus Christ. It's always appropriate to ask, what would Jesus do? This approach helps us to understand why God allowed many things in the Old Testament that Jesus forbids in the New, such as polygamy, deceit, oaths, and divorce.

Questions

1. If we dwell in the Word, and let the Word speak to us in our situation, it will form our lives. The Word shapes us. As we learn to live within God's Word, we find Scripture begins to "read" us rather than our reading the Scriptures. But that takes time. Is this true in your life? Is the television/internet/sleep, etc. more important than God's Word?

2. If you don't love God's Word the way you would like to or the way you believe you should, sincerely ask the Holy Spirit to give you a love for his Word. He will do it. David says, "Oh, how I love your law! I meditate on it all day long." (Ps. 119:97, 119:20).

3. Share an experience when God's Word changed your life.

4. Do you memorize God's Word? Do you agree that since Jesus and the New Testament writers often gave the essence of the Word, you can memorize it using this approach?

5. Read and compare different versions. Pray for God to open your eyes to his truth. You will find fresh food for your soul every time.

6. Paul writes that we are to be transformed by the renewing of our minds. (Ro. 12:2). David writes we are to store up God's Word in our hearts. (Ps. 119:11). Make these Scriptures real in your walk with Jesus.

6

Jesus' Mission is Empowered by the Holy Spirit

Jesus said, "Very truly, it is for your good that I am going away. Unless I go away, the Advocate will not come to you, but if I go, I will send him to you." (John. 16:7).

After Jesus' resurrection he breathed on the disciples, "Receive the Holy Spirit." (Jn. 20:23). Before he ascended, he "gave them this command: 'Do not leave Jerusalem, but wait for the gift my Father promised, … John baptized with water, but in a few days you will be baptized with the Holy Spirit.'" (Ac. 1:4-5). We don't need to wait ten days, but we must have the power of the Holy Spirit or we are helpless. We need God's Word empowered by the Holy Spirit if we are to "bear much fruit." (Jn. 15:5).

A Holy Spirit Deficit Disorder

The church today is suffering from a Holy Spirit deficit disorder. The American church has neglected the importance of the Holy Spirit. If we have a charismatic speaker, a talented worship band, or a flashy children's and youth program, we can draw a crowd and persuade people to respond to commit to church membership. That's a far cry from making disciples!

Concerning the churches in the United States, a Korean Pastor commented, "It's amazing what you people can do without the Holy Spirit." A. W. Tozer is reported as saying, "If the Holy Spirit were removed from the churches in America on Saturday, most would go on the next day as if nothing had changed."[36]

Hudson Taylor wrote, "We have given too much attention to methods and to machinery and to resources, and too little to the Source of power, the filling with the Holy Ghost."

> Surrounded by the self-sufficiency of American culture, we can convince ourselves that we have what it takes to achieve something great. In our churches we can mimic our culture, planning and programming, organizing and strategizing, creating and innovating—all in the effort that will show what we can accomplish in our own ability....
>
> But there is the way of Christ. Instead of asserting ourselves, we crucify ourselves. Instead of imagining all the things we can accomplish, we ask God to do what only he can accomplish. Yes, we work, we plan, we organize, and we create, but we do it all while we fast, while we pray, and while we constantly confess our need for the provision of God. Instead of dependence on ourselves, we express radical desperation for the power of his Spirit, and we trust that Jesus stands ready to give us everything we ask for so that he might make much of our Father in the world...
>
> Would you say that your life is marked now by desperation for the Spirit of God? Would you say that the church you are a part of is characterized by this sense of desperation?
>
> Why would we ever want to settle for Christianity according to our ability or settle for church according to our resources? The power of the One who raised Jesus from the dead is living in us, and as a result we have no need to muster up our own might. Our great need is to fall before an almighty Father day and night and to plead for him to show his radical power in and through us, enabling us to accomplish for his glory what we could never imagine in our own strength.[37]

"In the West the gospel has been intellectualized to such an extent that there is almost no mention of true faith and trust in Jesus. Academic qualifications and speaking ability are held in high regard, while spiritual maturity, character and the call of the Holy Spirit have been diminished in importance and largely consigned to being irrelevant when it comes to God's work."[38]

When we sit at our leadership meetings trying to discern God's direction and draw our strategies, are we conscious of the Spirit's presence? Is that why our vision is so small and our goals are things we can do ourselves? The Spirit takes us out on a limb, a very uncomfortable place, but that's where the fruit is. Faith is spelled R-I-S-K. Fear is our powerful opponent, and it wins most of the time.

Oswald Chambers warns, "The great enemy of the Lord Jesus Christ today is the idea of practical work that has no basis in the New Testament but comes from the systems of the world. This work insists upon endless energy and activities, but not private life with God. The emphasis is put on the wrong thing."[39] We need to be driven by the Holy Spirit to love Jesus and to serve him, as he gives us the passion to make disciples.

The Prominence of the Holy Spirit in the New Testament

The early church saw the absolute necessity of the Holy Spirit. He is spoken of 27 times in the Gospels, 43 times in the book of Acts, and 30 or more times in the remaining books of the New Testament. Jesus was conceived (Matt. 1:18-20), baptized (Matt. 3:16), led (Lk. 4:1), empowered (Lk.4:14, 18), and raised from the dead by the Spirit (Ro. 8:11).

By the Spirit we are born from above (Jn. 3:3-6), led (Ro. 8:14), liberated (Ro. 8:2), empowered (Lk. 24:49), baptized (Jn. 1:23-34), sealed (Eph. 4:30), and anointed for service (Lk.4:18). He molds our character and produces fruit. (Gal. 5:22-23). He intercedes for us. (Ro. 8:26). He interprets Scripture. (I Cor. 2:13, Eph. 1:17). He convicts of sin. (Jn. 16:9, 14). He teaches, inspires our prayers, calls and commissions, gives gifts, and guides the believer. By his power, we put to death the habits and evil practices of the flesh. (Ro. 8:2). Since he does all these things, you would think we would depend on him more than we do.

Christ Removed the Curse, Enabling Us To Receive the Spirit

"Christ redeemed us from the curse of the law by becoming a curse for us… so that we might receive the Spirit through faith." (Gal. 3:13-14). Don't punish yourself when you blow it. Jesus already took your sin and its penalty, so don't cower as a slave. (Gal. 4:4-7). You are a son or daughter. Accept your position and act responsibly. You are not under condemnation. (Ro. 8:1). Nothing can separate you from God's love. (Ro. 8:39).

One of the most powerful manifestations of the Spirit in my ministry was at Capital Christian Fellowship. A number of first timers approached our facility, saying, "What is it about this place. It feels different. There is something going on here. I can feel the love." People were being saved almost every week. At one point there were baptisms almost entirely of adults, eight months in succession. It was common to see people standing in little groups after the worship, praying for each other. The congregation was animated. People were bringing their unsaved friends. The music took us into the presence of God, and the little children often danced. At times when I made a point in the message that seemed to clearly speak to the people, they would break out in applause. The joy of the Holy Spirit was contagious.

Bible Teaching Alone Is Not Sufficient

Bible teaching, in itself, will not transform us. The Holy Spirit must quicken the Word. "If you have the Word without the Spirit you will dry up. If you have the Spirit without the Word, you will blow up. If you have the Word illuminated by the Spirit, you will grow up."[40] The world has lost its faith, because the church has lost its fire! (Ro. 12:11).

"As the Spirit of the Lord works within us, we become more and more like him and reflect his glory even more." (II Cor. 3:18 NLT).

"There is no pattern in the way people receive the Holy Spirit. The one result in all instances of the outpouring of the Holy Spirit is the desire to follow Jesus and make Him known."[41]

It's Best If Jesus Goes to Heaven

Jesus stated that it was to our advantage for him to leave because he was sending his Holy Spirit. (Jn. 16:7). Most of us would rather have the physical presence of Jesus than the mystical presence of the Holy Spirit. As we mature in our walk in the Spirit, the supernatural becomes natural. There is no life that can compare with the fulfillment Jesus brings to us through the presence and power of his Holy Spirit. No drug can compare to the joy he brings. Like Isaiah writes, gladness and joy overtake me. (35:10 and 51:11). In Acts 13:52, the disciples were filled with joy and the Holy Spirit. I pray that you are experiencing his joy.

Be Filled with the Holy Spirit

We are commanded to be filled with the Spirit. (Eph. 5:18). This command is in the Greek present tense, which means we are to be filled continually. D.L. Moody is quoted to have said that the reason we need to be filled with the Spirit is because we leak. It's like eating a meal. A few hours later we want to eat again. Paul enumerates three results of being filled with the Spirit in verses 19 and 20: we have joy, a spirit of thankfulness, and an ability to live at peace with others. Again, he writes that God's Kingdom is not a matter of what we are eating or drinking, but of righteousness, peace and joy in the Holy Spirit. (Ro. 14:17).

Jesus said we are to continually and consistently ask, seek and knock, and he will give us his Holy Spirit. (Lk. 11:9-13). The Holy Spirit provides all the gifts we will ever need. As we live in the Spirit's fullness, the supernatural becomes natural. When we are walking in the Spirit, every person we meet is a divine encounter. Every thought we bring captive to Christ. (II Cor. 10:5).

The Holy Spirit gives witness to Jesus. (Jn. 15:26). Some ask, "If we lift up Jesus, do we need the Holy Spirit?" We are helpless to exalt Jesus unless we have the Holy Spirit. It's the Spirit who makes real to us what Jesus and the Father are doing for us and through us.

Walk in the Spirit

"No doctrine of the Bible, relating to the plan of salvation is more plainly taught or more wide reaching than that which concerns the union between Christ and his people."[42] This union is possible only through the Spirit. We are not under condemnation (Ro. 8:1); we are free from the law of sin and death (Ro. 8:2); we are co-heirs with Christ (Ro. 8:17); nothing can separate us from Christ (8:39); he is made to us wisdom, righteousness, holiness and redemption (I Cor. 1:30); we have the mind of Christ (I Cor. 2:16); we walk in victory (II Cor. 2:14); we are blessed with every spiritual blessing (Eph. 1:3); and we are seated with Christ (Eph. 2:6). In this world we are like Jesus. (I Jn. 4:17).

A young church planter asked, "What is the one thing you would recommend to someone setting out to start a church?" Neil Cole gave this advice: "Don't do anything until you are sure Jesus is with you. Like Moses, tell the Lord, 'I'm not going to take one step forward unless you go first.' And let that be true for the rest of your ministry! I recommend you put yourself in a precarious place where if God doesn't show up and deliver you, you're dead. ... Be angry with the fact that the world can ignore Jesus without fear of consequences.'"[43]

The Spirit Calls Forth Leaders

What difference would it make in your leadership activities, if the Great Commission was the ultimate goal of your leadership?

Healthy churches expect the Spirit to call forth leaders. In Numbers 11:16-17, the Israelites were grumbling against Moses. They wanted meat. "The Lord said to Moses: 'Bring me seventy of Israel's elders who are known to you as leaders and officials among the people. Have them come to the Tent of Meeting that they may stand there with you. I will come down and speak with you there, and I will take of the Spirit that is on you and put the Spirit on them. They will help you carry the burden of the people so that you will not have to carry it alone.'"

In Acts 20:28, the Holy Spirit set the elders in positions of leadership. It takes time to earnestly pray and hear from God. We tend to give polite overtures to the Holy Spirit and offer up perfunctory prayers. We must learn to depend on the Holy Spirit to call forth our leaders. More than half the pastors in the United States would leave the pastorate if they could find another job. Might they have missed the calling of the Holy Spirit upon their lives? At times the Spirit imparts gifts through the elders: "Do not neglect your gift, which was given you through a prophetic message when the body of elders laid their hands on you." (I Tim 4:14).

Indigenous Leadership

Calling leaders from outside the congregation is widely accepted in the United States. In many congregations that are making disciples who make disciples, leaders will rise up within the congregation. It usually takes two or three years for a leader from outside the congregation to gain the respect and trust of the people. Those who grow up within the congregation already have this trust. When we go outside the congregation, we often overlook the gifts within. Some will feel that they are not qualified, because they did not go to seminary. Seminary training is most helpful if the seminary experience can dove tail with the congregation being served.

When I graduated from seminary, I was a stuttering, insecure twenty-four-year-old. I was fearful, as I traveled to candidate at a church. What I didn't know was that their current pastor who was retiring had a severe speech impediment. The Holy Spirit knew I needed this helpful sign, calling me to serve this congregation of God's people.

The Spirit Gives Gifts

Twenty-five or more spiritual gifts are listed in Scripture. Paul lists five of them in Ephesians 4:11: apostles, prophets, evangelists, pastors and teachers. They are given to build up the body of Christ. All of them are in operation today. We must raise up apostles – those with vision and the perseverance to implement their God's given vision; prophets – those who hear from God and boldly proclaim his truth; evangelists – those who courageously share the Good News; pastors – those who feed the sheep; and teachers – those who give practical instruction for discipleship based on God's Word.

One of the obvious weaknesses in most American churches is that we load everything on the pastor. Where are the prophets, apostles, teachers and evangelists? They are in our midst if we have faith to call and empower them. Paul instructs Titus to appoint elders in every church. (Titus 1:5). The word "pastor" is only mentioned this one time in the New Testament, although "elders" is mentioned a dozen times. Until we spread the responsibility of equipping the saints for the work of ministry from the pastors to elders or mature Christians as Paul instructs the Ephesians church our churches will be weak.

Other gifts we need to utilize are set forth in Romans 12:3-8 and I Corinthians 12:7-11: service, encouragement or exhortation, giving, leading, administration, mercy, wisdom, knowledge and faith. Every church would agree that persons especially gifted with musical gifts enhances our worship. As every Christian utilizes their gifts given by the Holy Spirit the body will become mature making disciples.

Holy Spirit's Power Needed for Sharing Jesus

When Jesus promised the coming of the Holy Spirit, the promise was given for the power to witness to the ends of the earth. (Ac. 1:8). Unless we grow in our dependence on the Spirit, we will find sharing the Good

News a tiring burden rather than a joy. No one can convict a person of sin or save a single soul. This is the work of the Holy Spirit.

Holy Spirit perseverance will triumph. A person from the Buddhist religion came to our church, found new life in Christ and is now brining her supervisor who has been away from the church for many years. Her zeal encourages everyone in the congregation.

We are overwhelmed with all the needs in the world. It's only by the power of God working through us that we can do anything of eternal value. After Paul lists several gifts of the Spirit, he introduces a more excellent way. (I Cor. 12:31). This is the way of agape love, Christ-like love. This love only comes through the Holy Spirit. "I pray that out of his glorious riches he may strengthen you with the power through his Spirit in your inner being, so that Christ may dwell in your hearts through faith." (Eph. 3:16-17).

Love is the most excellent way. The fruit of the Holy Spirit is love. Whom does God want you to love today? Ask God to fill you with his Spirit. You will begin to experience God's resurrection power as you let fear behind and step out in faith.

Questions

1. Do you agree that the church today is suffering from a Holy Spirit deficit disorder? Do we take the Holy Spirit for granted?
2. The Holy Spirit is the only one who can transform a life. Since that is true, what is our part in leading a person to Christ?
3. Do you believe we have apostles, evangelists, teachers and prophets in our churches today? How would their help relieve the pastor of too much responsibility?
4. Do you believe there are many other Holy Spirit gifts besides those in Ephesians 4:11 such as the gift of intercession, music, administration, leadership, hospitality, service, mercy, compassion, etc. If so what can you do to help call forth these gifts to extend God's Kingdom?
5. When the Holy Spirit came in power at Pentecost and in the early church, the manifestations in some cases were dramatic. Are we afraid of being considered fanatical if we expect the Spirit to work in supernatural ways?

6. As you can tell, I love the statement, "The supernatural needs to become natural." Every person we meet, every conversation we have, every word we say needs to be directed by the Holy Spirit. (Jn. 5:19; 12:49-50; 14:31). Is this too radical? Discuss.

7

Jesus' Mission is Buttressed with Prayer

"Lord, break my heart with the things that break the heart of God." Bob Pierce

For the outward journey to be effective, you must give a higher priority to the inward journey.

Passionate Prayer

Prayer is developing intimacy with Jesus. Jesus was intimate with his Father. He did nothing or said nothing except what he saw the Father do or say. (Jn. 5:19; 12:49). He did only what pleased the Father (Jn. 8:29), and did not do his own will but the will of the Father. (Jn. 6:38). Because of Jesus' model, I try to pray daily that I would say only what the Father wants me to say, and how to say it, and to do not my will but only what pleases my heavenly Father.

Brad Brisco and Lance Ford quote Henri Nouwen: "The discipline of prayer is the intentional, concentrated, and regular effort to create space for God. Everything and everyone around us wants to fill up every bit of space in our lives and so make us not only occupied people but preoccupied people as well."[44]

"When we learn to regard prayer as the highest part of the work entrusted to us, the root and strength of all other work, we shall see that there is nothing that we so need to study and practice as the art of praying aright."[45] Prayer is an act of the will. The Holy Spirit will give us the passion to continually commune with our Heavenly Father.

Prayer and passion are couplets. A lack of prayer reveals our lack of passion and a lack of passion reveals a lack of prayer. Note the passion in these verses: "As the deer pants for the streams of water, so my soul pants for you, O God." (Ps. 42:1). "My soul is consumed with longing for your laws at all times." (Ps. 119:20). "I open my mouth and pant, longing for your commands." (Ps. 119:131). God rewards those who earnestly seek him. (Heb. 11:6). The prayer of a righteous man is powerful and effective. (Jas. 5:17). Elijah was a great man of God, but James reminds us that Elijah was a man just like us.

"Faith needs a life of prayer for its full growth. There can be no true prayer without faith... Prayer is also the way to more faith... It is in prayer, in the exercise of the faith I have, in fellowship with the living God that faith can increase. Faith can only live by feeding on what is Divine, on God Himself."[46]

"Prayer is not primarily God's way of getting things done. It is God's way of giving the Church 'on-the-job' training in overcoming the forces hostile to God. The world is a laboratory in which those destined for the throne are learning, by actual practice in the prayer closet, how to overcome Satan and his hierarchy. God designed the program of prayer as an 'apprenticeship' for eternal sovereignty with Christ."[47]

Pray for Workers

Jesus said, "The harvest is plentiful but the workers are few. Ask the Lord of the harvest, therefore, to send out workers into his harvest fields." (Matt. 9:36-38).

> How little Christians feel and mourn the need of laborers in the fields of the world... How little they believe that our labors-supply depends on prayer, that prayer will really provide the workers... How little the burden of the sheep wandering without a Shepherd is really borne in the faith that the Lord of the harvest will, in answer to prayer, send forth the laborers, and in the solemn conviction that without the prayer, fields ready for reaping will be left to perish. And yet it is so. So wonderful is the surrender of His work into the hands of His Church, so dependent has the Lord made Himself on them as His body, through whom alone His work can be done, so real the power which the Lord gives His people to exercise in heaven and earth, that the number of the labors and the measure of the harvest do actually depend upon their prayers.[48]

Intensity

In the garden before his crucifixion, Jesus "agonized" in prayer. (Lk. 22:44). Both Luke and Paul use the same Greek word "agoneeah," but it's translated differently depending on the context: to pray earnestly, to struggle, strive or agonize. Peter was in prison and the church was "earnestly" praying for him. (Ac. 12:5).

Paul writes, "I want you to know how much I am 'struggling' for you and for those in Laodicea, and for all who have not met me personally." (Col. 2:1). Paul agonized for those he never met. "Epaphras… is always 'wrestling' in prayer for you, that you may stand firm in all the will of God, mature, and fully assured." (Col.4:12-13). John Knox prayed: "Give me Scotland or I die."

Missionary Statesman Don Jacobs writes,

> We Christians discover that our most powerful weapon against Satan is fervent prayer. When I asked some Ethiopians why their church grew so much during their 10 years of severe persecution (1982-1992), they all responded: 'We learned to pray out of our desperation.' We might think that persecution produces growth. That might be, but the heart of the matter is that persecution drives saints to give themselves to imploring prayer, because they can simply do nothing about the situation. Churches around the world are rediscovering the mighty power of prayer. Entire congregations are praying aloud; all at once for a long time, praying fervently, begging in fact. They are experiencing the truth of Jesus' invitation to ask…to seek…and to knock… (Matt. 7:7).[49]

There is a relationship between fervent prayer and the intervention of angels. During a severe thunderstorm I lost control of my car as it hydroplaned toward a semi-truck. I shouted, "Jesus! Jesus! Jesus!" then felt an amazing thud. I believe an angel moved my car to avoid a fatal accident.

"You will seek me and find me when you seek me with all your heart." (Jer. 29:13). Jesus' brother James was nicknamed "James camel knees," because his knees were calloused from kneeling in prayer. Hannah prayed out of great languishing and sorrow and the Lord granted her request. (I Sam.15:30). Samuel begged and pleaded with the Lord, and the Lord defeated the Philistines. (I Sam. 7:9).

Those suffering in prison for our Lord tell us to pray that they will be faithful witnesses for the Lord, rather than to pray for their deliverance. Do we pray more for physical healing for ourselves and our friends than we do for the salvation of our lost neighbors? We all know which is the more important. On the other hand, too often we pray for the ability to accept circumstances, when we should be praying for the power to change them.

Praying Together

"We know that the early churches prayed together. After Peter was supernaturally released from prison, we read in Acts 12:12, 'He went to the house of Mary the mother of John, also called Mark, where many people had gathered and were praying.' They specifically were praying for Peter to be released from prison, but we can assume that prayer characterized the house church meetings..."[50] This account encourages me, because God answers prayers even when we do not have the level of faith we should have. They had faith to come together to pray, but when God answered their prayer, they were surprised.

The early church devoted themselves to prayer. (Acts 2:42). The followers of Jesus prayed for ten days awaiting the promised Holy Spirit. Our churches in the U.S. are not normally known as places of prayer. "When you read the story of the early church in the book of Acts, you see people for whom prayer was fundamental, not supplemental. Three times Luke tells us that the church was devoted to prayer. They were utterly dependent on God's power. Every major breakthrough for the church in the book of Acts came about as a direct result of prayer."[51]

Learn To Hear God's Voice

We must learn to hear the voice of God. Jesus said of the shepherd, "His sheep follow him because they know his voice." (John 10:4) Then he said, "I know my sheep and my sheep know me...They will listen to my voice." (v.10-14). Very seldom does the Spirit speak with a shout. It's usually the small voice deep within us. It's so easy to let our rational minds overpower it. Continually praising God and walling in obedience to his Holy Spirit will enable you hear his voice.

The primary way we hear God's voice is through Scriptures, as the Spirit enlivens his word to us. (Ps. 119:105). We also hear through the guidance of the Holy Spirit. The Spirit would not allow Paul to preach in Asia or

Bithynia. (Ac. 16:6-7). Then Paul had a vision of a Macedonian begging him to come. (v.9; also 20:22-23). Isaiah prophesied, "Whether you turn to the right or to the left, your ears will hear a voice…, saying, 'This is the way; walk in it.'" (Is. 30:21). The main reason we struggle to hear his voice is that we don't take time to be quiet and listen.

When David Yonggi Cho spoke to a gathering of pastors in the U.S., they asked him the secret of growing a large church. He said, "You pray and obey." He spoke some more, and they asked him again his secret of growing his church. He said, "You pray and obey." Finally at the end of the evening, they said, "Pastor Cho, you still didn't tell us how you grew such a large church." He wept and said, "You don't get it. You pray and obey."

Five or Ten Minute Devotional Time?

Heidi Baker, who assisted Mother Teresa, works among some of the poorest people of the world in Mozambique. She writes, "I have to spend hours every day alone with my Jesus. I must have his presence or I know I cannot survive. I am often on my face in His presence, so I stay hidden in his heart, soaking in the secret place. If you look into the eyes of Jesus and eat and fill that hungry place with Him every day then His passion is alive and burning in your soul."[52] David characterized himself: "I am a man of prayer." (Ps. 109:4).

"On numerous occasions preachers in China have traveled to a remote area to visit believers. Nobody is told they are coming. When the preachers arrive they often find the believers gathered, sometimes even in the middle of the night! When asked how they knew they reply, 'The Lord told us to get ready because you were coming at this time.'"[53] In other places, undercover agents were spying. The Lord told them to stop announcing the places and time of their meeting; instead trust the Holy Spirit to reveal the details to each person.

> All people are created to have an intimate relationship with God. This is evidenced by the deep longing within each of us to be loved, accepted and affirmed. God intends for this deep need to be met in Him alone, and He pursues us for a relationship of intimacy which should give us a deep sense of security, worth and belonging. Jesus lived and led from this relationship. Sadly, many leaders never experience this level of intimacy with Jesus and spend their lives

trying to find it. Their insecurities shape their leadership. They move and lead towards intimacy rather than living and leading from intimacy. (Lk. 10:38-42).

Leading towards intimacy focuses on performance instead of relationship. Martha was busy with "the preparations" … She found her significance in her performance. Leading toward intimacy focuses on the temporal instead of the eternal. Martha was concerned about the physical… Leading toward intimacy focuses on the many instead of the one. Martha was busy doing many things. … The result was distraction and worry. Mary chose what was best, a relationship with him. Intimacy with Jesus is not a task on our list of things to be done; it is the number one thing we should pursue. … Where do I find my significance, in my accomplishments or my relationship with Jesus?[54]

My roommate in seminary was from Ethiopia. He knew what it was to give extensive time to prayer. His holy habit both challenged and encouraged me.

"When a church… spends more time in consultation, planning and committee meetings than in prayer, it is a clear indication the members have lost touch with the supernatural and have ended up, in Watchman Nee's words, 'serving the house of God and forgot the Lord Himself.'"[55]

Fasting

Jesus fasted. (Matt. 4). The apostles, prophets and teachers in Antioch fasted. (Ac. 13:2-3). Daniel fasted. (Dan. 9:30). Jesus said, "When you fast…" not "if you fast." (Matt. 6:1). He said, "When the bridegroom is taken from them; in those days they will fast." (Lk. 5:35). In John 4:31-34, the disciples urged Jesus to eat, but he said he had food they knew nothing about. His food was to do the will of God and to finish God's work. In Matthew 17 the disciples were unable to remove the demon from the boy. Jesus reminded them this kind comes out only by prayer and fasting. (V.21 KJV).

Paul often told the Philippians, even with tears, that many live as enemies of the cross, their god is their stomach, all they think about is their appetites, their mind is on things of this world. (Phil. 3:18-20).

It's reported that at the Billy Graham World Congress of Evangelism, it was easy to tell who was from the United States as compared to those from other nations. After the long days of inspirational messages, those from other nations were asking, "Where can we go to pray?" while the Americans were asking, "Where is the nearest restaurant?"

Fasting is an indication that we are serious with God. We say "no" to our worldly desires so that our spirits can gain strength. Prayer needs fasting for its full growth. Through fasting, we cast away the visible. We need food. Satan tempted Eve with food. He tempted Jesus with food. In fasting Jesus triumphed. "It is only in a life of moderation, temperance and self-denial that there will be the heart or the strength to pray much."[56]

Peter Wagner writes,

> It's the part we play as the ground forces in God's battle plan. … The church is His army, and our fervent prayers open the windows of heaven.
>
> What did Daniel's prayer and fasting set in motion? In response, God sent Daniel His answer: heavenly hosts to the rescue. The angel said he had been dispatched the minute the prayer had started. Daniel started the battle by praying, pleading with God.
>
> The Lord sent an answer, and then Satan countered by sending an opposing force to interfere with God's plan. For 21 days the battle raged out of Daniel's sight. So the battle against the evil forces, in this case the prince of Persia, was obviously not Daniel's. Drake's Study Bible gives an interesting comment here: 'All wars lost or won on earth are results of wars that are won or lost by the heavenly army.' The battles are fought in the heavenlies, between Satan's angels and God's angels, not down here.[57]

There is a clear relationship between fasting and breaking the power of demonic forces against the church. Revival will not come to America apart from a renewal in the spiritual discipline of fasting.

The mission leaders of the Ethiopian Church designate one day a week for prayer and fasting. When they discontinued this practice, their work plateaued. When they revived this spiritual discipline, churches were again being planted and the work thrived. When I read of Christians in many countries where the church is invading Satan's territory, I am impressed with their faithfulness in spending time in prayer. It seems they give as much time to hearing the voice of the Lord as they do to strategizing.

Pray Big Prayers

In a survey, people were asked just before they died what they wish they could have changed in their lives. Eighty-four percent said they wish they would have pursued a dream or a desire to do what they longed to do, while sixteen percent responded that they regret doing what they did. If you are walking with God, the desires in your heart will line up with God's desires for you. Exercise faith, prayer, patience and persistence, and move ahead as God opens the door. Don't let fear hold you back. Jesus said of the man who buried his talent that it will be taken away, and the worthless servant will be thrown outside where there will be weeping and gnashing of teeth. (Matt. 25:26-30).

"It is my strong conviction that it is impossible to ask God for too much if our hearts and motives are pure, and if we pray according to the Word and will of God. Remember, it is a basic spiritual principle that whatever we vividly envision, ardently desire, sincerely believe and enthusiastically act upon will come to pass, assuming of course, that there is spiritual authority for it. It is this principle that is the foundation of praying supernaturally."[58]

How big is your vision? How big was Jesus' vision when he gave the Great Commission and said, "As the Father sent me, I am sending you"? E. M. Bounds wrote, "God shapes the world by prayer."

"David Brainerd prayed, 'Lord let me make a difference for you that is utterly disproportionate to who I am.' God has designed us to depend on his Word to lead his people in ways that are utterly disproportionate to who we are.'"[59]

Are we failing to act upon the sweeping authority God has delegated to us? Ezekiel writes concerning God, saying, "I looked for a man among them who would build up the wall and stand before me in the gap on behalf of the land so I would not have to destroy it, but I found none. So I will pour out my wrath on them and consume them with my fierce anger, bringing down on their own heads all they have done." (Eze. 22:30-31). God would have saved the nation if one person had interceded. "Go up and down the streets of Jerusalem…If you can find but one person who deals honestly and seeks the truth, I will forgive this city." (Jer. 5:1). God has not destroyed America, because there are persons who intercede for the nation.

Jesus desires us to pray big prayers. Listen to these comprehensive promises: "I tell you the truth, anyone who has faith in me will do what I have been doing. He will do even greater things than these, because I am going to the Father. And I will do whatever you ask in my name, so that the Son may bring glory to the Father. You may ask me for anything in my name, and I will do it." (Jn. 14:12-14). "If you remain in me and my words remain in you, ask whatever you wish and it will be given you." (Jn. 15:7). "In that day you will no longer ask me anything…, my Father will give you whatever you ask in my name…. Ask and you will receive, and your joy will be complete." (Jn. 16:23-24). If we line up our will with God's will, then we can ask whatever we desire and God will answer. If we believe these promises, prayer will be our main business.

Paul urged the church to pray: "I urge… that petitions, prayers, intercession and thanksgiving by made for all people – for kings and all those in authority, that we may live peaceful and quiet lives in all godliness and holiness." (I Tim. 2:1-2).

"God will do nothing in the realm of human redemption until the church accepts her responsibility and uses her privilege of intercession. If the church will not pray God will not act because this would abort His purpose to bring His Church to her full potential as His co-sovereign."[60] This is why John Wesley said, "God will do nothing but in answer to prayer." "God shapes the world by prayer. The more praying there is in the world the better the world will be, the mightier the forces against evil… The prayers of God's saints are the capital stock of heaven by which God carries on His great work."[61]

Why Is Participation So Poor When We Invite People To Pray?

Jesus said my house shall be called a house of prayer for all nations. (Mk. 11:17). It's clear one of the purposes of God's house is for his people to meet for prayer. Jesus also informed us what should be the emphasis of our prayers: for the nations. Our vision and our faith are too limited. Do we even pray for our next door neighbor, let alone the nations? Psalm 2:8 promises, "Ask me and I will make the nations your inheritance and the ends of the earth your possession." Lord, forgive our lack of faith and give us your vision for the world.

Americans think and act as if we have little need for God. Our next meal is in the cupboard, our highly trained doctors will find a pill to remove our pain, our house will withstand the wind, and if it should be destroyed, the insurance will come to our rescue. However, if the doctor reports that there's a brain tumor in our child or if our relatives are suddenly in serious condition from an auto accident, participation in prayer would greatly increase. It seems evident it takes hardships, suffering and persecution to wake us up.

Comfort Trumps People's Needs

"We see up close a propensity in our budgets to value our comforts over others' needs…. More than five hundred million people in the world are starving to death. They lack food, water, and basic medical care. Children are dying of diseases like diarrhea; many who live will suffer lifelong brain damage from early protein deficiency… Nearly one hundred fifty million children are orphans. Yet judging by what we hang on to in our churches, convenient programs and nice parking lots are still more important than such children and their families."[62]

The early church devoted themselves to prayer. (Ac. 2:42). Paul admonishes us to pray continually. (I Thess.5:17). "Jesus told his disciples a parable to show them, that they should always pray and not give up." (Lk. 18:1). We believe that more money, more possessions will give us fulfillment. Many of us are too busy – watching television, following sports, moonlighting, etc. We think we need new cars, houses, appliances, furniture, and clothes. We are so enamored with travel, pleasure, vacations, recreation and eating at the newest restaurant, that we have no time to pray.

Jesus Is Our Model

"Moses gave neither command nor regulation with regard to prayer; even the prophets say little directly of the duty of prayer; it is Christ who teaches us to pray."[63] Very early in the morning Jesus got up to pray. (Mk. 1:35). He often withdrew to lonely places and prayed. (Lk. 5:16). The disciples asked Jesus to teach them how to pray but never asked Jesus to teach them to heal, to perform miracles or to teach or preach. On one occasion they did ask him why they could not cast out a demonic power. Jesus replied that their faith was lacking, and that this kind comes out only by prayer and fasting. (Lk. 17:20). When Jesus asked them to pray for one hour, they fell asleep. (Mk. 14:37).

If we were given a choice between spending an hour in prayer or serving by giving ten hours to assist the needy, most Christians would choose the ten hours of service. Service is important. However, like Martha, we find it easier to serve than we do to pray. Why? True prayer requires faith. Jesus chided his disciples more than once concerning their lack of faith. Without faith we cannot please God. (Heb. 11:6). On the other hand, prayer is like putting a car in gear; don't pray unless you plan to obey.

Greatest Prayer Partners

Do we realize that our greatest prayer partners are Jesus and the Holy Spirit? What incentive this should give us to pray. "Jesus is able to save completely those who come to God through him because he forever lives to intercede for them." (Heb. 7:25, Ro. 8:35). The Spirit also "intercedes for us" in accordance with God's will. (Ro. 8:26-27). Remember to join up with Jesus and the Spirit as you pray.

In the Garden before the coming of the Holy Spirit, the disciples could not pray for one hour. After the resurrection Jesus breathed on them, "Receive the Holy Spirit." (Jn. 20:22). The Spirit changed everything. Now they obeyed Jesus and prayed for ten days. (Ac. 1:14).

Paul instructs us to pray for him to speak without fear. (Eph. 6:19-20). If Paul needed the prayers of God's people to speak fearlessly, how much more do we need them?

"The Moravians, who had their beginning under Count Zinzendorf, carried on a chain of prayer day and night which continued uninterrupted for 100 years. This was the beginning of the modern missionary movement."[64] We read of churches in the third world praying for hours. They have urgent needs: food, health and safety, as well as spiritual needs. We have so much. It seems the one temptation the church can't conquer is prosperity.

Neil Cole led a seminar of chosen church leaders in Japan. The Holy Spirit told him to come without an agenda except to pray.

> It was risky to show up with these dynamic Japanese leaders who do not have time to waste, at someone else's expense and tell them, "Oh, by the way, I don't have an agenda.... We will seek the Lord and wait until we know we have heard from Him because it is important that this work be His, not ours."... As we prayed the

Holy Spirit began to speak to us and our prayers became more and more impassioned. We began to confess the sins of the people of God... My friend ... was angry at the fact that the Japanese people can go through life and not see the real Christ; instead, they are in bondage to ignorance and sin. We were all connected to one Spirit, and with one purpose we sought the Lord on behalf of the people of Japan. It was overwhelming. We were weeping, begging God for the souls of Japan and not accepting anything less than a new breath of God on the people... I am convinced that a victory was won in the spiritual realm for the hearts and souls of the Japanese.[65]

Where Do We Begin?

We must repent of our indifference, our lack of zeal, and our lethargy. Make prayer a holy habit. When you get up, throughout the day, and before you fall asleep, talk with your heavenly Father. Pray for the needs: family, church family, the multitudes who are suffering physical privation, and for those who are being persecuted.

When persons express a disappointment or pain, instead of saying, "I will be thinking about you," we need to learn to say, "I will be praying for you." When you meet them again, ask how things are and humbly remind them that you have been praying for them. Most people are open to prayer and will be impressed that you cared enough to see if your prayers are answered.

I taught a seminary course on Congregational Revitalization with sixteen church leaders. One question kept emerging: "How can we keep our passion hot? How can our congregations both find and live out the passionate life God intends for us? How can we obey Romans 12:11, 'Never be lacking in zeal, but keep your spiritual fervor, serving the Lord'?" These leaders were saying their churches were lukewarm. They had money and did not need a thing, but Jesus said of the self-sufficient church in Laodicea, they were wretched, pitiful, poor, blind and naked. (Rev. 3:17).

After teaching this course, the Lord gave me a prayer that I have prayed daily for years: "Father, you sent your only Son for me, I don't have that passion. Give me your passion along with the wisdom and energy to put it into action. Jesus, you left heaven and were born to a virgin; you were rejected, dying on the cruel cross for me. I don't have your passion. Give me your passion, along with strength and wisdom to carry it out. Holy

Spirit, you left heaven in all its splendor to come and live in my sinful heart, now being made holy by your work. I don't have your passion. Give me your passion and the wisdom to put it into practice today."

It's Helpful When Others Audibly Affirm the Prayer

I find it helpful when others pray along with me and I pray along with them with audible words such as, "That's right," "Thank you Lord," "Yes, Lord," "Hallelujah" or "Amen." In I Corinthians 12:16, Paul reminds us that it is expected that we say "Amen" as prayers are being offered up to God. This indicates that we are in agreement, and where two or three are in agreement, God promises to answer. (Matt. 18:19-20).

Can you imagine David, Elijah, John the Baptist, Peter or Paul sitting still when they prayed? I think they often wept as they cried out to God. I find it interesting that nowhere in the 66 books of the Bible do we read that anyone closed his eyes to pray. In Acts 4:24, they lifted their voices together in prayer.

If we will humble ourselves, seek God's face, turn from our wicked ways (self-centered living), and turn to God in faith, he will hear from heaven, forgive our sin and heal our land. (II Chron. 7:14). J. Edwin Orr writes:[66]

> What is involved in this verse? As God requires us to pray, we must not forget what was said by Jonathan Edwards: "To promote explicit agreement and visible union of God's people in extraordinary prayer." What do we mean by extraordinary prayer? We share in ordinary prayer in regular worship services, before meals, and the like. But when people are found getting up at six in the morning to pray, or having a half night of prayer until midnight, or giving up their lunchtime to pray at a noonday prayer meeting, that is extraordinary prayer. But it must be united and concerted. A Baptist does not become any less a Baptist, or an Anglican less loyal to the Thirty-nine Articles, or a Presbyterian to the Westminster Confession. But they recognize each other as fraternal intercessors.

Lord, teach us to pray!

Questions

1. "As the deer pants for the streams of water, so my soul pants for you, O God." (Ps. 42:1). God rewards those who earnestly seek him. (Heb. 11:6). Do you earnestly seek him?

2. Elijah was a great man of God, but James reminds us that Elijah was a man just like we are. Do you need more faith to pray like Elijah? What will it take to move us to be people of faith and prayer?

3. We read of Christians in other countries who spend much time in prayer. Why is that true? What will it take to move us to that level?

4. We must learn to hear the voice of God. "His sheep follow him because they know his voice." (Jn. 10:4). "I know my sheep and my sheep know me…They will listen to my voice." (Jn. 10:14-16). Do you listen to God's voice?

5. Have you discovered the joy of fasting? What will it take for us to pray and fast for the needs in our families, our community and in our hurting nation and world?

6. Ezra writes, "If my people, who are called by my name, will humble themselves and pray and seek my face and turn from their wicked ways, then I will hear from heaven, and I will forgive their sin and will heal their land." (II Chron. 7:14) Will we claim this verse to pray for revival in America?

7. Paul admonishes the Thessalonians to pray continually. (I Thess. 5:17). Is that possible? (Zech. 12:10, Phil. 4:6, Ro. 12:12).

8. Acts 4:24, "They raised their voices together in prayer to God." Today when the Holy Spirit moves powerfully this expression of prayer is often practiced. Do you feel comfortable when everyone prays audibly simultaneous?

Part 3:
Our Mission

8

Why Don't We Share the Good News?

When Christ is our life, sharing the Good News is as natural as breathing.
Colossians 3:1-3.

If all that you gained from your salvation in Christ is something that you could hold to without passing it on, then it is not Good News. Because of what the Good News is, it will make you share it with others.

John Piper writes, "What should we be doing? It's simple – not complicated at all. Tell people the good news of Christ from a heart of love and a life of service! That's it!" The majority of followers of Christ agree with two-thirds of this statement. They agree we must have a heart of love, along with a life of service. But they do not agree on what "tell" means. Most would say you can tell without opening your mouth. They say, "It's not politically correct to share your faith." This results in a lukewarm Christianity that is a clear indication we do not take the Great Commission seriously.

If we knew the solution to curing cancer and didn't share it, we would be guilty of a criminal offense. We have the answer to life's problems. It is not right to withhold Good News from those who, according to Jesus, are going to hell without faith in Him. Only six percent of Christians make an effort to share their faith! What is holding back the ninety-four percent from sharing the Good News? Could our "closed mouth" approach be indifference or cowardice?

We Forget Who We Are

When we are born again, we are in God's family. If Christ is in us, as the New Testament reminds us nearly 200 times, why are so many Christians living in fear and defeat when it comes to obeying the Great Commission?

We neglect to share Jesus because Jesus is not our life and breath. (Col. 3:1-3). We are in Jesus and he is in us. (Jn. 15). When we are in Christ we are not under condemnation. (Ro. 8:1). Our guilt is gone, and we are free to walk and live as Jesus walked. (I Jn. 2:6). We don't share Jesus because we forget who we are.

Poor Self Image

I grew up in a home where the unwritten motif was, "God opposes the proud but shows favor to the humble." (Jas. 4:6). "Pride goes before destruction, a haughty spirit before a fall." (Prov. 16:18). I had a poor self-image because I wanted to do great things for God, which I confused with being proud. I thought of myself as a struggling sinner. The New Testament reminds us dozens of times that we are saints. In God's eyes we are holy. We are the people of God. Jesus has given us all authority and power.

When I retired from pastoring and served as overseer, I was scheduled to speak in many churches as a church consultant. I always prayed before I spoke, "Lord you have blessed me with growing churches, help me when I speak today not to come across as a braggart, or as one who has all the answers." As I was praying about this one night at two a.m., the Lord said to me, "Go in your study, check in Strong's Concordance the number of times we are told to be bold and the number of times we are told to be humble." As you can guess, we are told to be bold more often than we are told to be humble.

This experience helped me to share Jesus more freely and to speak with confidence in urging congregations to make changes that I knew would help them to be more effective in reaching people for Christ and in making disciples. About that time, I discovered Solomon's statement in Proverbs 28:1, "The righteous are as bold as lions." Lord, increase our boldness!

We need to be assertive to share the Good News, not passive or aggressive. The early Christians were bold. Peter and John said, "We cannot help but speak about what we have seen and heard." (Ac. 4:19-20).

Jesus Is Not in First Place

We don't share Jesus because we are not excited or thrilled about our relationship with Jesus. We are lukewarm. David Platt writes, "We look back on the slave-owning churchgoers of 150 years ago and ask, 'How could they have treated their fellow human being that way?' I wonder if followers of Christ 150 years from now will look back at Christians in America today and ask, 'How could they live in such big houses? How could they drive such nice cars and wear such fine clothes? How could they live in such affluence while thousands of children were dying because they didn't have food and water? How could they go on with their life as though the billions of poor didn't even exist?'"[67]

Our sports, televisions, iphones, cars, vacations, yes, even our daily food and constant eating, are more important to us than the mandate of the Great Commission. People move to get a better job. Seldom do we hear of people moving because God has called them to help a struggling church or to help plant a church. Until we fall in love with Jesus and his Word, we will not share Jesus from a heart of love. Until we feast on Jesus, we will not minister out of the overflow because there is no overflow. When we are filled with his Spirit, we have a song in our hearts and a spirit of thanksgiving that people notice. (Eph. 5:18-19). Jesus said that out of us will flow living water – even rivers of living water. (Jn. 7:38).

Many, it appears, have nothing worth passing on. There is no smile on the face, spring in the step, or song in the heart. It's incredible that we can posses the real thing and keep it to ourselves. No person is a fully devoted follower of Jesus unless he or she is reaching out to bring others into the experience of the joyful presence of Jesus. (Ps. 16:11).

We Have Lost Our Passion

Jim Morgan, writes:

> Passion is what we can't keep inside. It spills over and can't be contained. We love our kids – we can't help but talk about them. We love our favorite sports teams – we talk about them first thing Monday morning at the water cooler. Christians love God more than anything else – He should constantly be on the tips of our tongues. Our passion for the Lord should be evident to all those around us. *"Private Christian"* should be an oxymoron – our faith should pour out through every fiber of our being.
>
> That passion should extend to a sincere concern for those who

don't know the Lord. The fate awaiting those dying without Christ should compel Christians to set off on a rescue mission – to bring our family, friends, neighbors and coworkers toward Christ before it's too late. That sense of urgency should drive us to risk our reputations or even lives for the sake of sharing something so valuable with those at such great risk. (www.SermonCentral.com)

We Are Too Busy

We all have the same amount of time. We take time to do what is important to us. Most things we are doing we can keep on doing, but the key is to do them with those who don't know Jesus. When you go shopping, golfing, bowling, bike riding, to watch a parade, to attend a school concert or to a ball game, invite your prebeliever friends to go with you. Invite them to your backyard barbeque along with a few church friends. If they enjoy sports, invite them over to watch a game on television.

When you go on a service project like cleaning up after a hurricane, take them with you. Most prebelievers will be glad to help. Build relationships and share the Good News from a heart of love and a life of service.

Our Secular Friends Would Not Feel at Home in Our Churches

Imagine your Muslim friend invites you to the mosque. What is your gut reaction? *Would I be embarrassed? I don't know what to expect or do. Where do the women go during the service? Do I kneel when the other men kneel? What should I give in the offering, if they have an offering?* I had these questions and many more before I went to a Friday night service at a mosque.

Our secular friends have no idea what goes on inside a church building. Some have been there for a funeral or wedding, but that is different from a worship service. They think, *I would stand out like a sore thumb. I don't have a Bible and have no idea where to find anything in the Bible. When the pastor mentions the children of Israel, I look to see if Israel is sitting close to me. The pastor has a vocabulary unfamiliar to mine.* Words like benediction, invocation, bulletin, epistle, justification, sanctification and salvation are strange. The unchurched are uncomfortable, and we know they don't fit.

We can help them feel comfortable by building a trusting relationship with them. This takes prayer, time and perseverance. It's easier to take the prebeliever to a social event like a community event or banquet before you take them to a worship service. When you do invite them to church, explain in detail what they can expect when they come. Hopefully they will be willing to risk giving your invitation a try, especially if you invite them to go with you. Take them to a social function of the church before you invite them for a worship service.

Our Churches Are Focused Inward

Most churches are ingrown and provincial and accept this as normal. Check out most weekly church programs and you'll find their activities are inside the four walls. Check the budgets. Most of the funds, usually 90 percent or more, are allocated for members rather than for those outside the church. We reason that, after all, members pay the bills, so why shouldn't the money be allocated for those who provide the funding.

Churches that are internally focused often become lethargic and discouraged because they are doing laps, running in circles, keeping the Good News to themselves. Their people slowly drift away, while those who remain are not enthusiastic enough to invite others to join them.

A healthy, externally focused church is a healthy church inwardly. These churches give members a sense of accomplishment. They know they are making a difference in individuals, in families and in the life of their community. Families are being healed instead of broken apart through divorce. Lives are being transformed for Christ.

Someone wrote, "A live church is seeking out sinners; the real calamity for a church occurs when it becomes full of 'nice' people on a 'nice' street in a 'nice' part of town." A nice church that neglects those on the margins will not be effective in making disciples who make disciples.

Most People Don't Want To Hear

Some people don't share the Gospel because they think people don't want to hear it. That's true for many, but Jesus reminds us that some seed will fall on good soil and bring a bountiful harvest. (Mk. 4).

When you make an effort to share the Good News but see no fruit, and perhaps even outright rejection, the devil immediately says, "You'll never be a good witness." Don't listen to the devil. God calls us to be faithful in sharing the Good News. He will give you other opportunities, in fact, many, many opportunities. I find God gives me opportunities daily, in the natural flow of life.

Lois, a vivacious second grade teacher who was just baptized, entered my study and said, "I can talk about everything in the teacher's lounge, but when it comes to sharing Jesus I am tongue tied. Why is that?" Our culture has taught us that religion is an individual matter. We invade people's territory when we share our faith. We don't like rejection. Nearly every page of the New Testament reminds us that our faith is not readily accepted by the masses of people. (Matt. 7:13-14). The devil will do all he can to discourage you from sharing your faith. We know the cross demands that we die to self and make Jesus Lord of our lives. We know the cross is offensive to all who believe they are good people and have no need to confess any sin.

Our grandson lived in Morocco for a time. Whenever he went outside, people met him and said, "Hi, how are you?" Next they asked if he was a Muslim. When he replied that he was a Christian, they immediately said, "Why aren't you a Muslim?" What a contrast from our American culture! Here was an open opportunity for him to share his faith.

Many Turned Off

When we moved to a new community, my wife Helen spent time with our neighbors, showing love and sharing the difference Jesus makes in her life. However, she felt checked by the Holy Spirit that now was not the time to confront one neighbor concerning her relationship with God. My wife found out later that a person had knocked on her neighbor's door and asked if she was a Christian. She said, "No." He told her she was going to hell. She said, "When I heard that a preacher was moving across the street, I was angry. But Helen, you are different. No matter what I say or do, you just accept me. Maybe Jesus will accept me too." Over the next months, she and her family accepted Jesus and worshiped with us.

Sometimes we are turned off by the way some people witness, telling ourselves we never want to be like that. However, can you name one person who has come to Christ by those who think it's not cool or politically correct to share your faith in Jesus?

There is nothing new about the gospel turning some people off. It was so in the New Testament and it is so today. It's also true that some seeds will find the good soil. Since we are Jesus' ambassadors, we must sow the seed and represent our King. Jesus said we are to compel them or make them come to the heavenly banquet. (Lk. 14:23).

There Is an Offense to the Gospel

The only obstacle people should experience in coming to Christ is the offense of the cross. The cross demands that we swallow our pride and say, "Yes, I believe Jesus is the Son of God and that he died for my sin." Pride is the president of hell. Repentance is the most difficult exercise we will ever do.

A major problem is the Gospel message. It doesn't resonate for people for whom life is providing their basic needs as well as many of their wants. Most in our American society are enjoying some success and pleasures of a wealthy culture. Even when there is a crisis as a job loss, divorce, major illness, or a serious accident where a person is injured for life, they know or believe that somehow the safety net will be there so they shrug it off, bite their lip and go on.

When there is a crisis, they blame it on the government, their employer, everyone or everything but "me." Multitudes, at least those above thirty-five years of age, know about the Gospel message but have rejected it as not being necessary or relevant for them. Jesus told us in the final days that hardness of heart will increase. Only the Holy Spirit can soften the heart. We need to be there when the heart is softening.

Some Believe There Are Many Ways to Heaven

Today studies show that fifty-six percent of evangelical Christians believe that there are many ways to heaven. If there are many ways to heaven, there is little if any need for passion to share the Good News and make disciples. Jesus made it clear that he is the only way. Jesus said in John 14:6, "I am the way and the truth and the life; No one comes to the Father except through me." Peter and Paul state clearly, "Salvation is found in no one else, for there is no other name under heaven given to men by which we must be saved." (Ac. 4:12). "God...wants all men to be saved and to come to a knowledge of the truth. For there is one God and one mediator between God and man, the man Christ Jesus." (I Tim. 2:5).

Some Believe There Is No Day of Reckoning

Craig Groeschel writes,

> I believe one of the main reasons people don't share their faith in Christ is that they don't really believe in hell... Research shows that while almost three out of four people believe in heaven, less than half believe in hell... If hell didn't exist, unbelievers would easily reject Christ with no fear of God whatsoever, and believers would be unmotivated to share their faith with nonbelievers... God has created a universe with a heaven—and a hell... We are here to help others come to terms with reality... When was the last time you were so burdened for someone far from God that you spent the whole day or night praying on their behalf? How many people have you brought with you to church?... When was the last time you had a non-Christian in your home? Is there someone in your family who doesn't know Christ... an old friend, a neighbor, or someone at work?

> If we truly understood what hell was like, we'd be much more motivated to help people avoid going there. Hell is a place of unspeakable suffering. Jesus says in Matt. 5:29, 'If your right eye causes you to sin, gouge it out and throw it away. It is better for you to lose one part of your body than for your whole body to be thrown into hell.' Can you imagine gouging out your own eye? According to Jesus himself, as horrible as it would be, digging your eye out would be far better than being punished for your sins in hell... The Bible calls hell a fiery furnace, a place of burning sulfur, the outer darkness, and a place where there is weeping and gnashing of teeth.[68]

Some say, "Now Is Not the Time"

Some say, "Now is not the time; I must learn to know my neighbors better before I share Jesus with them"; or "I must build my relationship a little longer. Now is not the time." These are valid concerns, but don't keep using them. If you do, you will never get around to sharing Jesus with anyone.

Multitudes who have attended church all their lives keep using this excuse. You know exceeding more than your neighbors and friends who don't go to church. Even very few college graduates know anything about the Bible. Don't let their education intimidate you. Don't hide behind this excuse.

We Fear Being Called a Hypocrite

This excuse will always be a temptation because none of us are perfect. Closely related is, "My life is not consistent with my message; they wouldn't believe me." Be humble and confess that you fall short many times. Unbelievers will understand and respect you if you are honest with them about your walk with Jesus. Confess any hypocrisy and don't hide behind your inconsistencies. Be transparent.

Some Fear Rejection

Did some reject Jesus? Absolutely! Are you better than Jesus? "They might laugh or make fun of my efforts." Think of what Jesus went through on the cross and realize your "persecution" is nothing compared to his suffering for you. Remember, the sufferings of this life are not worth comparing to the rewards of heaven. (Ro. 8:18).

You are responsible to share the Good News in a humble, respectful way. You are not responsible for their reaction to Jesus or to you. Let the Holy Spirit work with that.

I'm an Introvert

Don't use your shyness and discomfort as an excuse for not sharing your faith. Such excuses didn't work for Moses or Jeremiah. (Ex. 3:11, Jer. 1:6). If sharing the Good News is new to you, it will be uncomfortable at first. That will change. You will experience people who sincerely thank you for caring enough to share your faith with them. The Holy Spirit is a spirit of power and courage, and he lives in you. In fact, if we do not have the Holy Spirit, we are not Christians. (Ro. 8:9)

I Don't Have the Gift of Evangelism

Many say, "I don't have the gift of evangelism. I'm not a missionary." They think I'm not selling my house and leaving my family and friends. I can't learn a new language. My children would have to adjust to a new culture. The Great Commission does not mean I must pull up stakes and move to a foreign country. But the Great Commission is for every follower of Jesus! Begin by reaching across the street and across the water fountain at work, to the new student in school or the new neighbor who just moved into your community.

David Platt writes,

> "We take Jesus' command to make disciples... and say, 'That means other people.' But we look at Jesus' command in Matthew 11:28, 'Come to me, all you who are weary and burdened, and I will give you rest,' and we say, 'Now, that means me.' We take Jesus' promise in Acts 1:8 that the Spirit will lead us to the ends of the earth, and we say, 'That means some people.' But we take Jesus' promise in John 10:10 that we will have abundant life, and we say, 'That means me.'" [69]

Don't be guilty of claiming Jesus' promises selectively.

I Don't Want to Turn People into My Projects

Sometimes I hear, "God doesn't want us to make people into projects." Of course not! However, Jesus said we are to compel or make people come to the heavenly banquet. (Lk. 14:23). Again he said, "Follow Me and I will make you fishers of people." (Mk. 1:17). And in Matthew 28:18-20, "Go into all the world and make disciples."

The solution to moving from making a person a project is to show them sincere self-sacrificing love. The Holy Spirit's love comes with wisdom, with sensitivity to the person's needs and feelings. We fish, we urge, we compel, we invite under the leading of the Holy Spirit. Jesus compels by his extravagant love, and we can do no less. He had an agenda, and we must have one too.

I've Tried and Failed

If you believe that you are responsible to bring people to Jesus, you will fail. That's the work of the Holy Spirit. We are in an independent society where people do whatever they want. Many will not care what you say, some will frown, and others will yawn, giving you a "who cares" response. When that happens, thank them for their time and move on to others.

One man said to me, "I've invited my coworkers to church, and they didn't come. What more can I do?" As we will see in the next chapter, we must make many contacts and be persistent in building meaningful relationships before the prebelievers take us seriously.

Prayer, persistence and patience are the keys. Ask others to pray for you. If they are sincere, they will ask you how things are going. Report to them your progress or seeming lack of progress. Gentleness and loving persistence are absolutely necessary. Add patience and passion to your efforts, and remember God's word will never return void or empty. (Is. 55:11).

I Don't Have a Passion for the Lost

Many who claim to be followers of Jesus would rather have a root canal than share Jesus with their neighbors or peers. Passion grows out of a life of prayer.

> We must have a passion for the lost. I am not talking about merely having an interest in the salvation of sinners. No! I am talking about an all-consuming passion. I am not talking about subscribing to a program to evangelize people. No! I am talking about a life style through which we devote every ounce of our energy to winning the lost. This is not something with which we are born, not something that can be learned. It has to be imparted by the Holy Spirit. To receive this, we need to go to God in full repentance to plead for an impartation of His heartbeat for the lost. In II Peter 3:9, we read that God is patient toward us (the believers), not willing that any (of the unbelievers) should perish, but that all should come to repentance.[70]

Matthew Parris, a professed atheist, wrote,

> The New Testament offers a picture of a God who does not sound at all vague to me. He has sent his son to Earth. He has distinct plans both for his son and for mankind. He knows each of us personally and can communicate directly with us. We are capable of forming a direct relationship, individually with him, and are commanded to try. We are told this can be done only through his son. And we are offered the prospect of eternal life--an afterlife of happy, blissful, or glorious circumstances...

Friends, if I believe that, or even a tenth of that... I would drop my job, sell my house, throw away my possessions, leave my acquaintances and set out into the world burning with the desire to know more, and when I had found out more, to act upon it and tell others.[71]

Jim Denison writes,

Charles Spurgeon: "If sinners will be damned, at least let them leap to hell over our bodies. And if they perish, let them perish with our arms about their knees, imploring them to stay. If hell must be filled, at least let it be filled in the teeth of our exertions, and let not one go there unwarned and unprayed for."

Suppose Pope Francis devised a cure for all cancer, a remedy for AIDS and Alzheimer's and heart disease, a solution to radical Islam and the immigrant crisis, an end to all war and suffering. All of that, combined, would not be as eternally significant as helping a single soul find eternal life.

Sharing God's word is not imposing your opinion on others. It is offering those with a terminal disease (sin) the only cure (salvation). Is there a greater gift you can give today?[72]

Witnessing to Everyone

How can I witness to everyone? Paul writes in Acts 20:24, "I consider my life nothing to me; my only aim is to finish the race and complete the task the Lord Jesus has given me – the task of testifying to the good news of God's grace."

Perhaps Eugene Peterson, in translating the Message Bible, took liberty in translating this verse. He writes, "What matters most to me is to finish what God started: the job the Master Jesus gave me of letting everyone I meet know all about this incredibly extravagant generosity of God." While we may not discern that the Holy Spirit wants us to verbally witness to everyone we meet, like Paul we must never be ashamed of the Gospel of Christ, for it is the power of God that brings salvation to everyone who believes. (Rom. 1:16). Paul was not intimidated, knowing he was going to the capital of the Roman Empire.

The Holy Spirit will give you discernment when to speak. The Father told Jesus what to say. (Jn. 12:49). The KJV reads that not only did the Father tell Jesus what to say but also how to say it. Peter admonishes us to answer everyone with gentleness and respect. (I Pet. 3:15).

Don't Be Intimidated

Don't be intimidated. Paul reminds us, we are only servants. (I Cor. 3:5-10). We each have our part to do. Paul planted, Apollos watered, but God made the seed grow. So neither he who plants nor he who waters is anything but only God who makes things grow. In verse 10, Paul reminds us of our responsibility to be expert builders. There is this balance that only God can make the seed grow, but we have our part to sow the seed. Verse 9 says we are God's fellow workers; we are God's field, God's building. God will do his part. The question remains, will you do our part?

We never know how the Holy Spirit will use what we share to remind the unsaved of their need for Jesus.

Many Encounters Are Usually Needed

People seldom come to Jesus on our initial invitation. Passion and perseverance like Paul expresses in Romans 9:2-3 are needed: "I have a great sorrow and unceasing anguish in my heart. For I could wish that I myself were cursed and cut off from Christ for the sake of my brothers, those of my own race."

During the 1990's, studies indicated that it often took eight, ten or more contacts before persons opened their life to Christ. Today it will usually take more. Prayer, perseverance and God's love expressed in acts of kindness are crucial. The ladder of relationship puts this in perspective.

Ladder of Relationships:

Contacts
Acquaintances
Responders
Converts
Disciples

As I met Reba for the first time, she indicated to me that she would come to church. This was a green light, but I had to stop back nearly a dozen times before she came. She usually was not home, but I left our church program and wrote a note on it. Then I saw her mowing the lawn. She was delighted to see me and promised to come to church. She did and has come most every Sunday since. Now she's bringing her brother, her friend and has volunteered to teach the small children. Persistence is a must!

Where are the Evangelists?

"It was he (Christ) who gave some to be apostles, some to be prophets, some to be evangelists, and some to be pastors and teachers, to prepare God's people for works of service, so that the body of Christ may be built up until we all reach unity in the faith and in the knowledge of the Son of God and become mature, attaining to the whole measure of the fullness of Christ." (Eph. 4:11-13).

Paul instructed young Pastor Timothy to *do the work of an evangelist.* (II Tim. 4:5). Certain persons have the gift of evangelism. However, as I mentioned before, there are twenty some gifts mentioned in the New Testament, but when the opportunities present themselves, we all need to step up to the plate and do the best we can, no matter if we have that particular gift or not. As we exercise our gifts, they will develop. Jesus had all the gifts and as we grow in Christ-likeness we too can develop the gifts. Certainly the Great Commission is for everyone.

Why don't we recognize the gift of evangelist? We call teachers, ushers, custodians, secretaries, elders, librarians, trustees, pastors, video and audio engineers. The Ethiopian Church calls evangelists before they call a pastor. Gift discernment surveys reveal that approximately ten percent of Christians are evangelists. Since we don't recognize this gift or affirm these evangelists among us, few exercise this gift.

In Acts 8:4, everyone who was persecuted departed from Jerusalem and preached the word wherever they went. Philip was one of seven deacons and also an evangelist. (Acts 8; 21:8). Were the four men who carried the paralytic and lowered him through the roof all evangelists? Someone had to take the initiative to bring the paralytic to Jesus. At least one had the gift of evangelism. Perhaps the other three had the gifts of mercy, helps, service or administration. (Mark 2:1-12).

What are the characteristics of an evangelist?

- They love everyone, especially people on the margins. This means they often bring the "wrong" kind of people to church, which may result in being misunderstood and given a cold shoulder by some.
- They are likely loners in our nurture-focused congregations. Most evangelists will eventually leave a nurturing-focused church and find another church where their gift is used.
- They quickly bring a conversation to personal salvation.
- They exercise a holy boldness. They are people of faith. They expect results and have an untiring urge to share the Good News.
- They pray for their unchurched friends by name.
- They love to distribute invitations in the community and share the Gospel at nursing homes or in prisons.

You will do the evangelists and your church a tremendous favor if you spot these persons and encourage them. Tell them you are praying for them. If you care for their children so they can lead a Bible study with unchurched mothers, your reward will be just as great as theirs.

Should we recognize these persons publicly, or would that tend to give the other ninety percent another excuse to not share the Good News? While I did not publicly recognize these persons I would say to them privately, "You are my evangelists. Thanks much. I'm praying for you."

We Haven't Learned To Share Our Faith with Other Christians

One of the biggest reasons we don't share our faith with the unchurched is that we have not learned to share our faith with other Christians. When we meet other Christians, we're free to talk about everything but our faith. We talk about the weather, our new car, the stock market, our jobs, children, activities, or church problems. How often do we share how good God has been to us, or a particular Scripture that came alive during our quiet time, or an answer to prayer? Do we ask other Christians to pray for needs in our lives or the lives of our family? Rather than talking about how terrible the weather related disasters and criminal news reports are, encourage each other to pray for workers and for the people impacted by the devastation. The devil knows if he can keep us from sharing the goodness of God with one another, we will likely not be sharing the Good News with the lost. (Heb. 10:24-25; Ro. 12:10; 15:14).

The East African revival which began in the 1950's and is still going today was centered on two questions that they asked each other whenever they met: "How is your relationship with Jesus?" and, "How is your relationship with your spouse?"

In Conclusion: Driven by the Holy Spirit

The secret of removing the fear and hesitancy of sharing Jesus is to ask God to give you his passion for the lost, just as the Father gave Jesus his passion for humanity. This passion took him to his death. God has given us the keys of the Kingdom of Heaven. What an opportunity we have to bring people to God's Kingdom – to share the irresistible story of Jesus. It's a matter of life or death.

Questions:

1. What excuses do you give for not sharing the Good News more than you do?
2. What excuses do others in your church give for not opening their mouths to share God's love?
3. Give some illustrations of persons you encounter who are prebelievers, and tell why they have not come to faith in Christ.
4. Do you know people who are turned off by Christianity? Explain why this is so prevalent today.
5. Would your secular friends feel at home in your church? If not, why not? Is it because of the offense of the Gospel or is it another reason?
6. Why don't most people, especially the younger generation, feel guilty about sin? What will it take to change this?
7. The only obstacle people should experience in coming to Christ is the offense of the cross. Do you agree? Why is the cross so offensive?
8. Can you name some of the evangelists in your church? How can you have them utilize their gift more effectively?

9

Helpful Principles for Sharing the Good News

There Is No Greater Call, Privilege or Opportunity than Sharing the Good News

Our son, Chet, shared this when he introduced a message:

> My desire is that we represent Jesus proudly and well, so others can experience the awesome privilege of becoming part of God's family. His greatest, most urgent message for us is to communicate his Good News, joyfully, persuasively and effectively.
>
> It's incredible that as we partner with God, we can witness to new life in Jesus, coming alongside others so that, by his grace, we can not only dramatically change people right now today, but make the difference in where and how they will spend eternity. There is no greater call, privilege or opportunity.

Why does God leave us here after we become his disciples? Why doesn't he take us to heaven immediately? In heaven we can worship, fellowship, sing, pray, and hear God's Word, but we can't fulfill the Great Commission in heaven. That's why we are here.

Focus on the Person's Need

Jesus used a different approach with everyone he met, because their needs were all different: to Nicodemus he said, "You must be born again." To the woman at the well, "I'll give you living water." To Zacchaeus, "I'll come to your house." To the rich young ruler he said, "Sell what you have and give to the poor and you will have treasures in heaven." To the adulterous woman, "Neither do I condemn you, leave your life of sin." To the man who was blind from birth, "Do you believe in the name of the Son of Man?" To the demoniac who begged to follow Jesus, he said, "Go home to your own people and tell them how much the Lord has done for you, and how he has had mercy on you." (Mk. 5:18-20). Jesus saw people's needs.

Be Gentle and Respectful

Peter reminds us to answer people with a gentle and respectful tone. (I Pet. 3:15). We may have our facts right, but we lose our effectiveness if we are not courteous. Just as we like to be respected, we must respect and value others if we want them to listen to us.

Sharing the Good News is all about relationships. If people don't like you, it will be almost impossible for them to be attracted to Jesus. The best way to bring people to Jesus is to have intelligent, caring conversations with them. This opens the door to their hearts.

Serving others will soften their hearts, but they still need to experience more than loving service. Anyone, Christian or non-Christian, can serve because it doesn't take God's Holy Spirit to serve. The working of the Holy Spirit is necessary to draw people to the Savior and to make disciples.

In I Peter 3, Christians were in the pressure cooker, they were being persecuted. Peter reminds them to answer people with a gentle and gracious tone even in their extremely difficult circumstances.

In Colossians 4:6, Paul writes that we are to be wise in the way we act toward outsiders, making the most of every opportunity. Be gracious in your speech. Let your conversation be always full of grace, seasoned with salt, so that you may know how to answer everyone. The goal is to bring out the best in others as we talk with them; not put them down, but bring them hope. Our conversation should be "seasoned with salt," that is, it should be "tasty" so it encourages future dialogue.

Move Outside the Four Walls

Jesus was with people in the flow of society. Forty-five of his fifty-two parables were given in the marketplace. All but ten of his encounters recorded in the Gospels were outside the synagogue or temple. We will win very few to new life in Christ inside the four walls of our churches. That's a real challenge for so many church-going Christians and even a greater challenge for most pastors.

Scott, our oldest son, volunteers time to build bridges in Central America though the "Bridges Without Borders" organization. He purposely chose this secular organization to share the Good News with those he is serving, as well as those who go with him to build bridges. In helping to raise funds for these projects, he was invited to speak at a sports bar. He was introduced by the person saying, "He's a Christian, but he is okay."

Ron works in a plant where the men get together to eat their lunch. When he joins the group, the conversations change. Sometimes they call him "preacher," but he has earned their respect and is a faithful witness.

"T.W. Manson, in writing about how Christianity conquered the Roman Empire in the first three centuries says, 'When we try to picture how it was done, we seem to see domestic servants teaching Christ in and through their domestic duties, workers doing it through their work, small shop keepers through their trade rather than the eloquent propagandists swaying the mass meetings of interested inquirers.'"[73]

Everyone Needs Purpose and Satisfying Relationships

People need purpose and hope. The United States is in the top third of the nations for people who commit suicide. Nearly one-half million people attempt suicide each year. The leading cause of suicide attempts is hopelessness. People feel lonely, alienated, and lack meaning in life. Jesus offers the antidote to all of these. The church must be a loving community. God is love. As Rick Warren says, "We are commanded to love God and to love one another fifty-five times in the New Testament."

One main reason for such a high suicide rate in financially prosperous countries is the inequality of wealth. Usually, the larger the gap between the rich and poor, the more frustration and anger there is, which often results in criminal acts. Through television, the poor see what possessions the opulent have, so they feel deprived. Their wages, if they are fortunate enough to have a job, are only a fraction of those around them. In the poorer countries, they may not have access to television and those in their communities are living in poverty just as they are. Thus the social pressure to move up the financial ladder is not as great.

Introduce people to a life of purpose and satisfying relationships. Ideally, you can verify these wholesome and healing relationships in your church. Our fast paced world and modern technology also contribute greatly to depression and despair. We don't allow ourselves time to meditate. Iphones, tablets, television, and internet remove us from healthy face to face relationships. Relationships can easily grow cold without face to face contacts. Nearly half of the children with iphones experience some form of depression. Jesus calls us to a deep personal life of love with himself and with others. Healthy churches live out the 17 "one another" commands in the New Testament, thereby providing a haven for those who are lonely and depressed. (See Chapter 13 for more on the "one another" commands.)

Let Others Help You

In Luke 10, Jesus sent 72 disciples out two by two. When we invade the Devil's territory, instead of going alone, it is wise to take another Spirit-filled Christian with you. Satan is often like a roaring lion, and he is not to be taken lightly. (I Peter 5:8). Discouragement can set in quickly when you are alone. We need the wisdom, prayers and encouragement of others. Anytime you witness for Jesus, try to have someone praying for you and for the individuals you are witnessing to. In Colossians 4:3-6, Paul asks for prayer that God will open the door, so he can proclaim the mystery of the Gospel clearly. He was aware of the necessity of including others to assist in his witness. We too need the prayers and support of others as we share the Gospel.

I have a close friend born in Africa who has participated many times in using the Luke 10 approach of sending out pairs as lambs among wolves. Missionary teams have been successful using this approach in many countries. While this approach may not work in our context in the United States, the principles are evident. We are not to depend on our education, training, money or personal charisma but on the Holy Spirit to know when and how to share God's love.

What Is the Good News?

The Gospel is something we announce. In Luke 2:10, the angel appeared to the frightened shepherds and said, "Do not be afraid. I bring you good news that will cause great joy for all the people." Other translations read, "I announce to you" or "I have good news for you." The Greek word for "announce" or "bring" is the word we translate evangelism. When we bring good news of Jesus, we are evangelizing. Who doesn't want to hear good news!

The Gospel is an announcement of an event that really happened. It has to be announced. By God's Holy Spirit we live out its implications, but if we're to make the gospel known, we must use words. A godly life should bear witness to this event. If we live the life but never share the event, we call attention to ourselves. People see us and do not see Jesus, unless we tell them about his incarnation, crucifixion and resurrection. A godly life cannot communicate the Good News by itself. Verbal communication of the gospel is the only means by which people are brought into a right relationship with God.

To the Romans (10:9-14) Paul says, "If you declare..." (or confess – "confess" is more than a cognitive exercise saying "I have sinned"). "If you declare with your mouth, 'Jesus is Lord' and believe in your heart that God raised him from the dead, you will be saved. For it is with your heart that you believe and are justified, and it is with your mouth that you profess your faith and are saved... For everyone who calls on the name of the Lord will be saved. But how can they call on the one they have not believed in? And how can they believe in the one of whom they have not heard? And how can they hear without someone preaching to them?"

To the Corinthians he writes, "I want to remind you of the gospel I preached to you which you received and on which you have taken your stand. By this gospel you are saved, if you hold firmly to the word I preached to you. Otherwise, you have believed in vain. For what I received I passed on to you as of first importance: that Christ died for our sins according to the Scriptures, that he was buried, that he was raised on the third day according to the Scriptures, and that he appeared to Cephas, and then to the Twelve." (1 Cor. 15:1-4). The Good News must be spoken, but if we don't hold on to it or live it, we believe in vain.

The Apostle John puts it in these words: "He who has the Son has life; whoever does not have the Son does not have life." (I Jn. 5:12). John 3:36 is almost identical: "Whoever believes in the Son has eternal life, but whoever rejects the Son will not see life, for God's wrath remains on them." Jesus prayed, "This is eternal life: that they know you, the only true God, and Jesus Christ, whom you have sent." (Jn. 17:3). The Greek word "gnoridzo" that we translate "know" is experiential knowledge not simply a cognitive exercise.

In our American context, "believe" simply means intellectual assent. So often I talk with people who say things like, "My husband believes in God, he just doesn't go to church." My spirit says, "Even the demons believe and shudder." (Jas. 2:19). Belief must include active obedience. (Ro. 16:26). Explain "believe" as the Amplified Bible does: "believe means to trust in, cling to and rely upon the fact that Jesus is Lord." (Jn. 3:16).

What Do I Share? The Focus Is on Jesus!

We share Jesus! Philip told the Ethiopian the Good News of Jesus. (Ac. 8:35). "Paul witnessed from morning till evening, explaining about the kingdom of God... He tried to persuade them about Jesus." (Ac. 28:23). Jesus is God's Son who died on the cross for my sins and arose again. He is now in heaven. If you believe and trust in God to save you and repent of your sin, he will forgive you. The Good News is that God accepts you. Are you ready to receive his acceptance and live in union with God? Too often our attitude is condescending. "You the unsaved are on the outside, I'm on the inside. I'll tell you how to get inside if you want." Jesus reached across – not down! "The Word became flesh and moved into the neighborhood." (Jn. 1:14 Msg.). (See Chapter 10 for other ideas on how we can best share the Good News.)

It's Easier To Talk about God as Compared to Jesus

Jesus' name is powerful. We can't remain neutral. We must either accept or reject his claims to be the unique Son of God. It is much easier to talk about God than about Jesus. Jesus warned us that all people will hate his followers because of him. (Lk. 21:17). Even though atheism and agnosticism are making rapid advances in our culture, the paradox is that the majority of people when faced with a major crisis still accept the possibility of God or a god. They see Jesus as a specific god set apart from other gods, so therefore they see those who believe in Jesus as narrow-minded.

Our salvation is in Jesus alone; therefore as we share the Good News, we must move from God to faith in God's Son Jesus, who is the only one who can remove our sins. (Ac. 2:38; 4:12).

The Necessity of Repentance

One of the serious mistakes we have made is that we have neglected teaching the necessity of repentance. John the Baptist, (Matt. 3:2), Jesus, (Matt. 4:17), and Peter all began their ministry with a message of repentance. On the birthday of the church, Peter said, "Repent and be baptized in Jesus' name for the forgiveness of your sins." (Ac. 2:38). Paul writes, "I preached that they should repent and turn to God and demonstrate their repentance by their deeds." (Ac. 26:20).

Repentance is necessary not because we earn God's blessing by repenting, but we must be humble to receive the grace of God. We must admit we are sin-sick, and then God will grant us grace. (I Jn. 1:9). It's the same principle with churches. The church cannot turn around and move from an internal focus to an external focus unless it is willing to (repent) make changes.

Repentance is an ongoing process since sin is an ongoing condition. After thirty years of being in the church, Jesus' message to the people in five of the seven churches in Revelation 2 and 3 was a message of repentance. (See Chapter 3.) How often do you hear James 4:9-10 preached today? "Grieve, mourn and wail. Change your laughter to mourning and your joy to gloom. Humble yourselves before the Lord, and he will lift you up."

Fifty percent of adults in the United States claim to have prayed to Jesus and think they are going to heaven, even though there is no discernible difference in their lifestyles from those outside the church. Because there was no sincere repentance, there is no lasting major transformation.

Don't Use the E-Word

The term "Evangelism" is repulsive to most Christians and judgmental for the unchurched. I try not to use the word. Use positive nomenclature, e.g. share the Good News or share how you found satisfying purpose, meaning and joy in the Lord.

Witnesses Not Attorneys

Jesus calls us to be witnesses not attorneys. A witness shares what he or she has seen and experienced. We are not to argue with anyone, but be like Peter and John who said they could not help speaking about Jesus. (Ac. 4:20). The blind man had a powerful witness by sharing, "Once I was blind but now I see." (Jn. 9:25). Jesus reminds us that if we acknowledge him before others, he will acknowledge us before our Father in heaven; but if we disown him, he will disown us. (Matt. 20:32-33).

Stay Away from Denominational Identity

Corrie Ten Boom says that, to the unchurched, denominations are like firemen arguing over which color of fire hose to use while the building is burning down. We need to work together even though we do not see eye-to-eye on every detail of doctrine. Christians can differ on less essential issues (e.g. mode of baptism, method of church organization, worship styles or eschatological positions), while cooperating to do evangelism and ministry together.

To the unchurched and to the dechurched, denominations smack of provincialism, being closed-minded, narrow-minded, or intolerant. Why would they want to join a group that argues over non-essentials? To Generation X'ers the church is even looked upon as dangerous. Today's culture questions all institutions. Not mentioning denominational identity doesn't mean you have to abandon your identity with your denomination. Emphasize that your church is all about Jesus whose central teaching is to love God with all our heart, soul, mind and strength and to love our neighbor as we love ourselves. Our congregation emphatically repeats, "It's not about you. It's not about me. It's all about Jesus!"

Walter Lewis, the personal secretary to C. S. Lewis, remembers Lewis saying, "Imagine a spaceship landing right here before us and a group of Martians walking out and greeting us. Imagine they say to us, Now we only have a few minutes before we have to return to Mars, so please don't mind our frightful appearance. We hear you have some Good News. We would very much like to hear this before returning home. Can you tell us about it?

And you know what would happen, don't you? Surely someone would speak up and say, Well yes, this church over here, they have liturgy, but the other church in town does not. And that church over there, they have candles, but the first church I told you about, they do not…and what would happen? Well, the Martians would return home having not heard the Good News….

Lewis believed we are far more concerned with church format and denominational differences than we should be. What we should be concerned about is the real matter before us: sharing the Good News."[74]

Do We Ever Give Up on People?

Today many people have experienced rejection by the church. When we show genuine Christ-like love, some will risk trying the church once more to find healing. Once people leave your church, it will be very difficult to win them back. Often, it's best to encourage and bless them to seek another church that may better meet their needs. For many, especially of the younger generation the attraction model will not reach them. Building relationships is a must.

When the rich young ruler turned away from Jesus, Jesus did not go after him. Neither did the Father pursue the Prodigal Son but waited until he came to the end of himself. Paul was fearful of wasting his efforts on the Galatian Christians. (Gal. 4:11).

"John" had several bad experiences with churches. He was lonely and found friends at our church. Day after day, he vented his anger from previous hurtful times. We listened to his derogatory statements too long. Some people who came to visit the church were turned away because of his disparaging comments and obnoxious behavior. Like Pharaoh, his heart was hardened. When he left, it was a blessing. We can't reach everyone. We pray John finds healing before he dies.

Fishermen

When Jesus calls us, his call is the same for us as it was for Peter and Andrew: "Come follow me, and I will make you fishers of men." (Mk. 1:17). Jesus wants to make something of us. Our lives are going to influence men and women for eternity. Someone has said, "If you are not a fisher of men I don't know who you are following, but you are not following Jesus."

When Jesus called James and John, they were washing their nets. (Mk. 1:19). Many Christians have become professional net washers. We talk about fishing, attend classes to study fishing techniques, listen to lectures presented by fishing "experts," but do we actually fish? When we follow Jesus he makes us fishers of people. If a fisherman never casts out his net to catch fish, is he truly a fisherman?

We Are All Called To Witness

Paul instructed shy Pastor Timothy to do the work of an evangelist. (II Tim. 4:5). Philip, a deacon, was an evangelist. Evangelists are to work along with prophets, apostles, pastors and teachers to equip the church so that it moves from infancy to maturity. (Eph. 4:11-15). These Scriptures give the impression that certain persons have a special gift, which is true. However there are twenty some gifts mentioned in the New Testament; but when the opportunity presents itself, we all need to serve, show mercy, teach, administrate, give and witness. The Great Commission is for everyone.

Jesus' last words are unmistakable: "You will receive power when the Holy Spirit comes on you, and you will be my witnesses." (Ac. 1:8). God has no "Plan B." Jesus says you must do the witnessing. You will receive power to witness. The "you" is plural; that means every disciple. Where you witness is in Jerusalem (at home), in Judea (your neighbors), in Samaria (your enemies), and around the world. Jesus says, "You will be witnesses," not you might be; we must share Christ with our world.

The Fish Are Plentiful

Jesus said the harvest is ripe and plentiful. In every community there are a majority who don't know Jesus! No community of any size or county in the United States has a church attendance above twenty percent. In many cities it does not reach ten percent. That means that eighty percent or more of the people in our communities are not involved in church. If you meet a dozen teenagers on the street and ask them if they have ever been to church, on the average only one will say he or she has been inside a church building. We have no choice but to go outside our church walls, build relationships, and invite them to encounter Jesus and his church. Remember, we don't clean the fish before they get into the boat.

By way of contrast, there are 100,000 to 170,000 being baptized every day around the world. It's the greatest time in history to be alive. So don't be discouraged.

Practice What You Preach and Preach What You Practice

Sometimes you hear, "Preach the Gospel; if necessary, use words." Francis of Assisi was to have said this, but that is not true. In fact he often preached five times a day. This statement, while well intentioned, is not Biblical. As

Christians, we should live so that our lives model Jesus' life. But can I live such a perfect life that people will come to Jesus without them hearing the Good News? That's not possible! Even Jesus' perfect life would not be sufficient to give us eternal life without him telling us how to receive salvation.

Ed Stetzer quotes Mark Galli: "'Preach the Gospel; use words if necessary' goes hand-in-hand with a postmodern assumption that words are finally empty of meaning. It denigrates the high value that the prophets, Jesus and Paul put on preaching. Of course, we want our actions to match our words as much as possible. But the gospel is a message, news about an event and a person upon which the history of the planet turns."[75]

The gospel without words is incomplete. It's an event that must be proclaimed. That proclamation is done through words. These words taken seriously transform our lives. But even a transformed life in itself will not explain how to find salvation.

We have all heard, "Practice what you preach." James writes, "Do not merely listen to the word, and so deceive yourselves. Do what it says." (Jas. 1:22). We say, "Actions speak louder than words." We want people to know where we get our strength to go through tough times. We want our prebelieving friends to experience the hope, joy and peace Jesus gives us. This means we must live the story and tell the story. That means we must not only "practice what we preach," but preach what we practice.

Confusion Between Proclamation and Social Action

The Gospel is words and deeds; Good News and social action. "The trouble with the social gospel, even when it is clothed in religious garb and operating within Christian institutions, is that it seeks to fight what is basically a spiritual warfare with weapons of the flesh. Our battle is not against flesh and blood or symptoms of sin like poverty and sickness. It is against Lucifer and countless demons who struggle day and night to take human souls into a Christless eternity... The accent must first and always be on evangelism and discipleship."[76] It sounds too brash, but the church often sends people to hell. We educate, we fill their stomachs, and we try to give them everything we know as the good life, except they are lost without knowing Jesus. When will we make the first thing the first thing?

Today, Service Trumps Evangelism

Jesus kept service and evangelism in balance. It's the truth that sets people free. Our good works won't set them free. No one is saved because we treat them nicely. It is the Gospel, the Good News, that brings people to Jesus. Today, service trumps evangelism. This takes away the uncomfortable feeling most have with verbalizing the Gospel. Multitudes of Christians fall into that trap. The world just loves it when we serve them without sharing the Good News. But our good works do not bring them to salvation, unless we tell them why we are letting our light shine.

Proclamation Is Our Primary Task

Proclamation is the primary task of the church. We come to church to worship God and to encourage one another, but the primary task is to proclaim the Good News extending God's Kingdom. A godly life serves as a witness for the message. Without words, our actions point to ourselves. We can't be good news, but we can explain, sing, speak and preach the good news to anyone who will listen.

Paul makes this clear: "Everyone who calls on the name of the Lord will be saved. How can they call on the one they have not believed in? And how can they believe in the one of whom they have not heard? And how can they hear without someone preaching to them?" (Ro. 10:13-14). Preaching necessitates using a language. As I said in Chapter 1, preaching is primarily for the prebelievers, not for those who have a salvation relationship. Once a person is walking with Jesus, they need teaching to equip them to move to maturity in Christ.

Today's church too often pushes to the back burner the fact that Jesus came to save sinners. We can devote ourselves to feeding the hungry and clothing the naked, thinking we have fulfilled our assignment. We fail people when we give them bread but keep silent about the Savior who can meet their true needs, fill their deepest hunger, and heal their greatest hurts.

Demonstration Is Important

We must demonstrate the Gospel as well as proclaim it. "Do not merely listen to the word, and so deceive yourselves. Do what it says." (Jas. 1:22). People listen with their eyes. Some will want to know the hope we have. They're not very concerned about our doctrine. Salvation is about a relationship with a person, not a set of rules and regulations. Jesus said to the Jewish leaders, "You study the Scriptures diligently because you think that in them you have eternal life. These are the very Scriptures that testify about me, yet you refuse to come to me to have life." (Jn. 5:39-40).

People should be coming to you and me asking, "What is it about you that makes you do what you do? You are different." (I Pet. 3:15). That doesn't happen to me as often as I would hope. My wife Helen on many occasions has been asked, "What makes you different? You live with pain every day, and yet you are vivacious." A college professor shared with me how his students continually ask him why he is different from the other professors. He frequently stays after class and individually assists those who need extra help. What a powerful witness.

We Have a Poor Image of the Church

We can't win people to Jesus and make disciples if we have a poor image of Christ's church. The church is the Body of Christ. How we feel about the church has a direct bearing on our love for Christ, the head of the church. You can't love the one without loving the other.

The church is the best we will ever have. The Government, the military, our educational systems, or even the Red Cross can't bring lasting transformation to the hearts of men and women in our communities.

Millions of dollars are poured into various rehab programs. The results are very meager. There must be more than a social gospel to bring about life transformation. Only Christ Jesus is the center and solution of all lasting transformation. Our churches should be like a hospital emergency room.

"The church is meant to be a training center and command hub for war, not a social club for pleasantries and hypocrisy, where people give lip service to Christ while refusing to obey His commands... Quantity isn't as important to God as quality. He doesn't need an army of people to accomplish His purpose. Just a few obedient servants with the anointing of the Holy Spirit can bring about great things for God."[77]

Notice these military terms which call for total dedication.[78]

- Put aside the deeds of darkness and put on the armor of light. (Ro. 13:12).
- Be on your guard; stand firm in the faith; be courageous and strong. (I Cor.16:13).
- God leads us in a triumphal procession. (II Cor. 2:14-16). Parades followed military victories. God enables us to triumph in our battles with Satan and evil.
- We use weapons of righteousness in the right hand and in the left. (II Cor. 6:7).
- We do not fight with weapons of the flesh. We use God's weapons for the destruction of Satan's fortresses. (II Cor. 10:3-4).
- We put on the full armor of God so that we can stand against the devil's schemes. For our struggle is not against flesh and blood, but against the rulers, against the authorities, against the powers of this dark world, and against the spiritual forces of evil in the heavenly realms. Therefore put on the full armor of God, so that when the day of evil comes, you may be able to stand your ground, and after you have done everything, stand. ... In addition, take up the shield of faith, with which you can extinguish all the flaming arrows of the evil one. Take the helmet of salvation and the sword of the Spirit, which is the word of God. (Eph. 6:11-18, I Thess. 5:8).
- Stand firm in one spirit, striving together as one for the faith of the gospel, without being frightened in any way by those who oppose you. (Phil. 1:27-28).
- Epaphroditus is a fellow soldier. (Phil. 2:25).
- Fight the good fight of faith. (I Tim. 6:12).

There are major differences between Christ's army and the military. The Christian army doesn't kill people; we battle with spiritual weapons. We do not have a rigid hierarchy. But all followers of Christ must be conscious of the battle and our need for vigilant discipline in our struggle with spiritual forces.

We Are on the Offense

Our focus is offense. We intentionally claim territory from the Evil One and free the captives. Jesus commissioned Paul: "I am sending you to the Gentiles to open their eyes and turn them from darkness to light, and from the power of Satan to God, so that they may receive forgiveness of sins and a place among those who are sanctified by faith in me." (Ac. 26:17-18).

Jesus said that the gates of hell will not overcome the church. (Matt. 16:18). The church empowered by the Spirit is stronger than Satan. He cannot overcome a Christian or the church, if our trust is in Jesus. We are sent to push back Satan's kingdom and to deliver any who are caught in bondage to his schemes. Don't be afraid to invade his territory. (I Jn. 4:4).

Jesus invaded the world's system to destroy the works of the devil. (I Jn. 3:8). We attack the devil's strongholds, releasing the captives. (II Cor. 10:4).

We are disciplined. "Endure hardship with us like a good soldier of Christ Jesus. No one serving as a soldier gets involved in civilian affairs - he wants to please his commanding officer." (II Tim. 2:3-4). "Train yourself to be godly." (I Tim. 4:7).

Do you see yourself as a soldier in daily battle? Do you see the need for a disciplined life, or are you like many American Christians living a soft, pleasure-focused life wondering why the church is so weak?

Training Is Hard

"Under the army metaphor, disciplined prayer becomes essential. We are called to work at prayer or 'struggle in prayer' as Paul puts it in Colossians 4:12 and Romans 15:3. We know we need to make regular times to gather for intercessory prayer. God answers these prayers. We deny ourselves, study the Bible, and go the extra mile to help our neighbor. People who understand the militant images in the New Testament no longer view assembling together as an option for weeks when they're not busy; instead they view the gathering and equipping as an important responsibility."[79]

War Is Harsh

Judy, whose husband is an alcoholic, called and pleaded with me to go to the bar and get her husband. I called a member who understood the bar lifestyle. We went and discovered the police had just left. They were mopping up the blood of someone who had just been shot. When you are on the front lines of God's army, life can be harsh. Personal sacrifice is a must to snatch people from the fire. (Jude 23). We are engaged in warfare for the eternal destiny of those on the way to hell. It's a matter of life and death!

Jesus Gives Us His Authority and Power
(Matthew 28:18-20, Acts 1:8)

When I was a substitute school teacher, the principal gave me the authority to enter the classroom and teach. But having the power or ability to teach is quite different. Jesus knew we needed both, so he gives his disciples the ability, as well as the authority, to witness for him in the world.

In John 17:18 and 20:21, Jesus says that as the Father sent Jesus, he sends us. Jesus could not be any clearer. We are sent! Did the Father send Jesus with insufficient resources? No! Just as our Heavenly Father sent Jesus, he sends us. We have all the resources we will ever need.

We are sent with the authority of Jesus every day until he returns. (Matt. 28:18-20). We have the power, the dynamic, and the ability given to us by the Holy Spirit. (Ac. 1:8). What more can we need or want? This Acts 1:8 promise is given in the context of sharing the Good News at home and around the globe. "He will never leave or forsake us." (Heb. 13:5). Jesus expects and empowers us to share the Good News. Too often we don't connect the dots between hearing the Good News and sharing the Good News.

You Can Hasten Christ's Return

In Matthew 24:14, Jesus said, "The gospel of the kingdom will be preached in the whole world as a testimony to all nations and then the end will come." Jesus is depending on you and me to carry out the propagation of the Gospel to the ends of the earth. Sometimes when Christians hear of so much widespread suffering and wickedness, they say, "I hope the Lord returns soon." Remember Jesus' admonitions to share the Good News to hasten his return.

Moved by Persecution

Jesus gave his followers this clear command to witness to everyone. Did they obey? No. They stayed home. It took persecution to move them. I am convinced it will take no less to wake us up. Persecution is at our doorstep. It will come in many forms. The secular culture may not be tolerant of Biblical teaching. We see this on many fronts today.

We will be pushed to privatize our faith. There may well be an economic meltdown, violence in our streets, government oppression, and disasters such as drought, hurricanes, floods, disease, famine and war.

Jim Denison, in his April 25th 2016, Denison Forum writes: "The Satanic Temple (TST) is a movement that began in 2013. The group now has seventeen chapters in the U.S. and Europe and claims an estimated 100,000 members. Its members have created satanic coloring book for distribution in Florida and Colorado schools. Offered prayers to Satan at a Seattle high school football game, and demanded that a satanic statue be erected next to a monument of the Ten Commandments at the Oklahoma State Capitol."

Jesus said in John 15:13, "Greater love has no one than this: to lay down one's life for one's friends." It cost Jesus his life, and it may cost us our lives. We must take up our cross and follow Jesus. He expects us to be the salt and light in our world. Suffering for Christ is a blessing. "For you have been given not only the privilege of trusting in Christ but also the privilege of suffering for him." (Phil.1:29 NLT).

We need the Holy Spirit for everything, especially for witnessing. (Ac. 1:8). Zechariah 4:6 reminds us, "'It's not by might nor by power, but by my Spirit,' says the Lord." Paul, in writing to the Corinthians, says that his words were not "wise and persuasive" but rather they were a "demonstration of the Spirit's power" in order that their faith "might not rest on men's wisdom, but on God's power." (I Cor. 2:4-5). Two chapters later, he writes, "The kingdom of God is not a matter of talk but of power." (4:20). The same Spirit that raised Christ from the dead is living in us. (Ro. 8:11).

Brother Lawrence, a seventeenth century monk, writes that he didn't worry about anything, and asked God for nothing except that he might not offend Him. He greatly disliked kitchen work, but that was the work assigned him. He learned to ask God for grace, and God always came through. His goal was to think of nothing but God. If he did allow some time to pass without thinking of God, he did not grow upset about it. He returned to God with all the more confidence and joy because he had found himself unhappy apart from God's presence. He wasn't afraid of anything, because complete surrender is the only secure road of indescribable joy.[80]

I was a shy, stuttering youth who often struggled in school, but by God's grace he enabled me to speak, not with arrogance but with humble boldness.

Only the power of the Holy Spirit makes that transformation possible!

I sell my books at a local flea market. Busloads of people come from many states. Motorcycles and tattoos are plentiful. Many of these people are not the least bit interested. It's only the Holy Spirit that gives me a holy boldness to experience rejection with joy and confidence to invite the next person to consider my books, which are full of Scripture. Paul wrote to Timothy, a shy, sickly pastor, "God did not give us a spirit of timidity, but a spirit of power, love and self-discipline. So do not be ashamed to testify about our Lord. Join with me in suffering for the gospel by the power of God who has saved us and called us to a holy life...." (II Tim. 1:7-9). Are you willing to recognize you have both the authority and power of the Holy Spirit within you?

Questions:

1. What is the Good News?
2. Is repentance necessary for salvation?
3. Discuss the statement, "Jesus calls us to be witnesses not attorneys."
4. Is it easier for you to serve others through acts of kindness than it is to verbally share Jesus? Will your acts of love and kindness bring people to salvation in Jesus Christ?
5. Is the image of the church being God's army one that resonates with you? Do you see yourself as part of God's army?
6. Do you see your church as part of God's army? What image would you use to describe your church?
7. What will it take to put you on the offense rather than being passive concerning sharing the Good News?
8. Is the Great Commission the primary focus of your church? Does your church budget indicate that this is your main reason for existence? Does the time commitment of your pastor indicate that this is his or her primary mission? Is this your primary mission?
9. Surveys clearly reveal new people bring new people. Surveys also indicate that the longer a person is a Christian the less they share the Good News. Why is that true?
10. Do you agree with this statement: If you do not love the Body of Christ, you cannot love Christ?

10

Sharing the Good News

Jesus said, "We are to compel them to come!" Luke 14:23.

You Can Do It!

Not only can we witness, but we can't help but witness. If Jesus is our life, (Col. 3:3), and we are praying continually with a joyful and thankful spirit, (I Thess. 5:16-18), our witness will overflow naturally. It's not a matter of "have to" – it's a matter of "want to" and "get to."

If a day goes by that I have not made people more aware of God, I feel I need to ask for God to forgive me because I missed an opportunity. I pray every day that I will not waste time, but that I will make good use of every opportunity, because the days are evil. (Eph. 5:16; Col. 4:5).

It's Simple

John Piper writes, "What should we be doing to help unbelievers be transformed into God's Kingdom people? It is simple – not complicated at all. Tell people the good news of Christ from a heart of love and a life of service! That's it! Tell people – open your mouth –tell ¬people the Good News – (Gospel) of Christ from a heart of love and a life of service. II Corinthians 4:5, what we proclaim to you is not ourselves but Christ Jesus as Lord and ourselves as your servants."[81]

The following illustrations are elementary, but even these elementary suggestions are off most Christians' radar screen. Unless you are a "God-conscious" person, you miss many opportunities of bringing God into the moment when meeting people.

Ways You Can Share the Good News

Weather

Since Americans are comfortable talking about the weather, I use the weather to introduce the God dimension. Such statements as "It's a beautiful day, God is good" and "We sure needed this rain; God sent it at just the right time," bring God to a conscious level. When there are storms and tragedies, we can make statements like, "We don't always understand the ways of God, perhaps he is trying to wake us up, (Luke 13:1-5), or maybe he is giving us the opportunity to help those who suffered from the storm."

God's Creation

David wrote, "Every cloud is a flag to God's faithfulness." (Ps. 108:4 Msg). "The heavens declare the glory of God; the skies proclaim the work of his hands." (Ps. 19:1). He calls the stars by name. (Ps. 147:4).

A soldier in France told the little peasant girl, "We will tear down everything that reminds you of God." She said, "You will let us the stars."

Natural revelation is a logical place to begin to introduce God's special revelation of his Son Jesus. It's God who created and sustains his creation. Don't let evolutionists spoof you into thinking everybody has bought into their philosophy. Use God's creation to open the door to introduce God as our creator. It's one way we can remind people that God is real to us and is as close as every tree, flower or bug. If God cares for the sparrows, certainly he cares for us. (Matt. 10:29-31). Thousands of times, and that's not hyperbole, we are reminded of God's creation as we read the Scriptures.

In fact, God makes it hard for us to go to hell. He is obvious, clearly seen in every flower, bird, tree and leaf, every newborn baby, every animal and insect. He is clearly seen everywhere. (Ro. 1:20). We don't take God to people, he is already there. We pray to be used to open their eyes so they can see him. God's creation is perhaps the most natural way we can help people think about God.

Paul writes, "This Gospel has been proclaimed to every creature under heaven." (Col. 1:23). How can that be true? Perhaps he is thinking of Psalm 19:1-4, "The heavens declare the glory of God; the skies proclaim the work of his hands. Day after day they pour forth speech; night after night they reveal knowledge. They have no speech, they use no words; no sound is heard from them. Yet their voice goes out into all the earth, their words to the ends of the world." "God's eternal power and divine nature is made plain to everyone because it is evident in his creation, so we have no excuse." (Ro. 1:19). "Jesus is the true light that gives light to everyone." (Jn. 1:9). We are all born with a sense of right and wrong.

In light of these Scriptures, pray for the eyes and hearts of those who have not accepted the Good News to be opened to God who surrounds them.

Daily News

Use the daily news to remind people that God is in control. The news is usually negative, but you can respond by commenting how good it is to know that God is in control and that our future is in his hands. When our economy is in a down turn, let's remind ourselves what Hebrews 13:5-6 says, "Keep your lives free from the love of money and be content with what you have, because God has said, 'Never will I leave you; never will I forsake you.' So we say with confidence, 'The Lord is my helper; I will not be afraid. What can man do to me?'"

"When the foundations are being destroyed, what can the righteous do?" (Ps. 11:3). "God reigns over the nations. He is seated on his holy throne." (Ps. 47:8). "He reduces the rulers of the world to nothing. The nations are like a drop in the bucket." (Is. 40:12).

It's a joy to remind people that we look forward to a better world. (II Pet. 3:11-12). Our citizenship is in heaven, and we eagerly wait for Jesus to return. (Phil. 3:20). Jesus will set everything right. When that happens, there will be no more bad news.

Religious Symbols

Many people wear an ornamental cross or other religious symbol but have no concept of the significance and gravity of the cross or of how Jesus expects us to daily shoulder our cross. I begin conversations by comments like, "I notice the cross you are wearing. How long have you been a Christian?" Or, "That's a neat necklace, you must be a Christian." Or, "I see you love Jesus." It's usually easy to move from these statements to more substantive dialogue. In most situations you know immediately if the person is serious about his or her faith.

Tattoos

People are willing to take the time and money to display their tattoos. They choose a particular tattoo for a reason and advertise it to the world; therefore it is not impolite to say, "I notice your tattoos. I'm sure you have them for a reason. I'd like to hear your story."

Finger Nail Art

Many women pay for nail art. As with tattoos, a woman has chosen a particular picture or design for a reason. Let her tell you the story behind her art. This is usually only appropriate for women to relate to other women.

Sports

Many people wear sport emblems or symbols. This is one of the easiest ways to open a conversation, especially with men, although more and more women are wearing these emblems also. I try to keep abreast of the sports world, so I can use it as a bridge to open a conversation and build a relationship. While it may not always be easy to transition from sports to faith in God, the Holy Spirit will often surprise you as he opens the door. You might ask if the person has children in sports and comment that it takes dedication and lots of time to take them to practice and pick them up. How do you find time for the family?

You can ask, "Who is your favorite player?" When the person tells you, you may respond, "I admire zealous athletes. In fact he or she reminds me of Paul the Apostle who said, 'Train yourself to be godly.' Paul used Olympic imagery. No half-way business with him. By the way, do you go to church? If they seem interested, sum up I Corinthians 9:24-27 in your own words. "Do you not know that in a race all the runners run, but only one gets the prize? Run in such a way as to get the prize. Everyone who competes in the games goes into strict training. They do it to get a crown that will not last; but we do it to get a crown that will last forever. Therefore I do not run like a man running aimlessly; I do not fight like a man beating the air. No, I beat my body and make it my slave so that after I have preached to others, I myself will not be disqualified for the prize."

Another verse you might use is, "Train yourself to be godly. For physical training is of some value, but godliness has value for all things holding promise for both the present life and the life to come." (I Tim. 4:7-8).

If you feel this is too assertive or if you feel uncomfortable, offer to go with the person to a game or athletic event to build a relationship, so you can eventually share Jesus.

Those Depressed or Discouraged

The October/November 2015 issue of the AARP magazine states that 50% of folks who are 40-59 years old say they are missing something in their lives. (p.86). As you talk with people and listen intently, many will share a problem. Rather than have an attitude of disdain, thank God for the opportunity to help. Their problems or needs are the open door for you to walk through to move them one step closer to Jesus. Paul reminds us that "to the weak I become weak." (I Cor. 9:22).

How do we become weak? When people share that their children are disobedient and getting into trouble, listen and respond by saying that your children have problems too. After you listen for a few minutes, you might gently and humbly mention that prayer has helped you and that you will be praying for them. In fact I have found most people are not offended if you pray for them on the spot. The Readers Digest reported that ninety-seven percent of people believe in prayer. You will find that as you pray, some will wipe away a tear. More importantly when you meet them or contact them again, ask how things are and mention you have been praying. If you can, help meet their need in some way. Trust God to give you the wisdom, strength and resources. Unless you are willing to make sacrifices, you will not win people to the Savior.

Reach across not down. God tried to reach down in the Old Testament by giving us the law, but we did not follow his instructions. In the New Testament, God gave us his Son who humbled himself and came in human form and reached across to us. (Phil. 2:6-8). He identified with our needs. (John 1:14).

Times of Change

During times of pain and change, people are usually more receptive to the Good News. These changes can be negative or positive: e.g. marriage, marriage crisis, divorce, first child, loss of a job, financial setback, sickness/hospital experience, death of a family member or close friend, a move, child in trouble, accidents, graduation or promotion.

Listen to their pain or enter into their joy. God gave us two ears and only one mouth; that should tell us something. We don't learn when we are talking. Listening is showing love. Everyone wants to be understood. Everyone deserves to be understood. Taking time and effort to understand another person is showing love.

As you empathize, the Holy Spirit will give you wisdom to know what your next response should be. Paul writes, "Each of you should look not only to your own interests, but also to the interests of others." (Phil. 2:4). Then he says we are to be like Jesus, who stooped to the lowest position and became a slave serving us. We must do no less.

Ask Questions

Sincere questions tell people we are interested in them. Ask questions and then listen. The Bible records more than 150 questions that Jesus asked. Matthew's Gospel alone records eighty or more of Jesus questions. Jesus knew the answers, so why did he ask questions? If we are to be a fisher of men as Jesus commands, we must catch their interest. If our questions are from a caring heart, they will build a bridge to open people's hearts to God.

Stay away from "why" questions until you have built a trusting relationship. Why questions can be threatening and usually make people defensive.

Ask questions that people can easily answer; questions that reveal something about them. Questions that can be answered with "Yes" or "No" are usually not helpful. Ask questions that only they can answer; for example: their name, what keeps them busy during the week, where they live, or questions about their family. These questions put them in the driver's seat. You are learning from them, and hopefully if asked in a loving respectful way, they will feel comfortable giving you the information. You are building a friendship.

How Are Things With You?

Perhaps the simplest approach is the sincere question, "John, how are things with you?" It's important to call people by name. It shows you care enough to learn their name. Listen and let the Holy Spirit guide you. This simple approach is effective not only with seekers but with followers of Jesus. We are too timid in checking with each other concerning our daily walk with Jesus.

What Are You Reading?

In an atmosphere like a coffee shop or waiting room, I have found that most people who are reading a magazine or a book don't mind you asking, "What are you reading?" They often love to tell you what they're reading. This opens the door for further conversation.

Children

David writes, "We're not keeping this to ourselves; we're passing it along to the next generation – God's fame and fortune and the marvelous things he has done." (Ps. 78:5-7 Msg).

"Jesus called the children to him and said, 'Let the little children come to me, and do not hinder them for the kingdom of God belongs to such as these.'" (Lk. 18:6).
Lois, Timothy's grandmother, and Eunice, his mother, passed on their faith to Timothy even though it appears that Timothy's father was not a believer.

Malachi closes the Old Testament with this warning: "I will send the prophet Elijah to you before that great and dreadful day of the Lord comes. He will turn the hearts of the parents to their children, and the hearts of their children to their parents; or else I will come and strike the land with total destruction." We see this prophecy being fulfilled today as fathers take their children to Sunday morning soccer games instead of taking their children to worship God. Over half the children in the United States do not have a father who has been with them for their first eighteen years. No wonder our prisons are full.

One of your greatest missions is to pass on your faith to your family. Your families are fertile fields for planting gospel seeds. In my many years of pastoral ministry, this is the way most people were able to transmit their faith. It was true in the New Testament and it is true today. You already have a natural bridge to your parents, brothers, sisters, uncles, aunts and cousins. Share your faith in Jesus. Be sure they see Christ's love, caring and joy in your daily life.

Today, most Christian parents place education and sports ahead of church activities. Church is not even on many Christian parents' radar screen. Is it any wonder most of our youth ignore the church? We say Jesus is important but our actions show differently. In all fairness many church activities for our youth are more focused on shallow entertainment which is little better than the world. Our focus must be on training our youth to be fully devoted followers of Jesus. We are satisfied if our kids are "good kids" who stay out of trouble. "Good kids" are a far cry from "Godly kids." Until we move from "good kids" to "Godly kids," there is little hope for making strong disciples to encounter our secular universities where the pressure is overwhelmingly geared toward seeing God as irrelevant.

Studies show that if children go to church, three percent of their families will follow; if mothers attend church, about twenty percent of families will follow; if fathers attend church, more than ninety percent of families follow. Churches must learn to appeal to men. Jesus is the "Lamb of God," but men also want to see Jesus as a "lion." Jesus stood up to the religious and political rulers of the Roman Empire. He cleansed the temple. He called Herod a fox. Jesus would not be intimidated by anyone. Pray for parents to become fully devoted disciples who lead the way for families to be transformed by Christ.

Food and Neighbors

Food is a leveler. Everyone likes to eat. Jesus' ministry was often centered around food. In fact, it seems Jesus is always eating with people. Luke pictures Jesus eating in eight of his 24 chapters.

Hospitality is one of the key gifts for fulfilling the great commission. Hospitality means "love of strangers." Entertaining, places the focus on the host. Biblical hospitality focuses on the guest. In Luke 10:38-42 Martha focused on entertaining Jesus while Mary was conscious of meeting the real desires of the guest. One of the qualifications of church leaders is that they must enjoy having people in their home. (I Tim. 3:2 and Titus 1:8).

Helen invited our neighbor women on our short street for an afternoon tea. They nearly all came. Two of them lived diagonally across the street, several houses between them, but had never met in seventeen years. They were amazed that we who were new in the community introduced them to each other.

Men are often more reluctant to come to a gathering where they don't know anyone. Invite the neighbors for desert or for burgers over a fire pit. This is less threatening. Lance Ford and Brad Brisco, on Forge Network suggest the following "rules" which they have found to work very well: You don't' need to bring anything or anyone, you can bring a dish or a beverage, there is no program, no agenda, just eat, talk, laugh and tell stories. No RSVP's necessary, all are welcome." You will be amazed at how many will respond. People are lonely and many will respond when invited to a non-threatening atmosphere with their neighbors.

Community Children

Most children in your neighborhood have no idea of the true meaning of Easter or Christmas. Many of their parents, who don't go to church, attended church when they were children; but their children have no understanding of the Christian faith. They have no concept of what the church is. Even though there are Christian radio and television stations 24/7, they do not tune into them.

Open your home for a Saturday morning Bible story time. Children will bring their friends. They are great missionaries.

With the parent's permission, you can take these children to church and to youth activities. Some children will persuade their parents to come if they are participating in a program. Most parents love to see their children participate; therefore intentionally design programs so it's natural for children to encourage their parents to come.

Can you coach a little league team? Your demeanor will be your primary witness, but having prayer before the game and having the team to your home following the games are settings where you can share the Good News. Take time to build relationships with children.

One church I pastored had a thriving Day Care, which opened the door for dozens of people to enter the church and find new life in Christ. Another church had an after school program, which also helped to bridge the gap between no faith and faith.

Summer Bible School continues to be an effective tool to reach community children. If efforts are made to visit and follow-up in the homes of unchurched children, some will be reached for Christ. Instead of having the Bible School in the church building we divided into several homes which made it easier for parents to invite their neighbor children.

People at the Checkout Counter

Compliment the clerks behind the counter on their efficiency, their patience with the customers who were ahead of you, or their friendly demeanor. On weekends, I often ask if they have to work Sunday. If they say yes, I say, "I'm sorry that means you have to miss church." If it is Monday, I ask if they had to work Sunday morning. This opens the door to talk about church. "I really miss it when I can't go. I hope you can find a good Bible believing church. Jesus makes a huge difference in my life." By going to the same checkout lane, you learn to know the clerk by name.

Standing in line, I love to get in conversations with people since they have nothing to do but stand and wait. Solomon says, "The righteous are as bold as lions." Many people have pets and of course buy pet food. Most any comment related to their pet food will open the door. People love to talk about their pets. A special sale is also an easy ice breaker.

Pets

Most people walking their dog appreciate any attention you give to their pet. Pray for the Holy Spirit to give you wisdom to bridge the gap from loving a pet to sharing the good news. You will be amazed as God opens your mouth to share the goodness of God with others.

Moving Vans

There are some things you don't need to pray about. Should you stop and meet your new neighbors in hopes of bring them the Good News? Don't give it a second thought – your answer is covered in the Great Commission. Rejoice when you see a moving van in your community. You can pray about what to say or what welcome gift you might take. After you introduce yourself and meet their family, ask if you can assist them in getting acquainted with school or local utilities in the community. If they don't have a church, you have an open door to invite them. Offer to take them and introduce them to your friends.

Real Estate Signs

When you see a real estate sign, pray for the persons who will be moving in; then when they move in, you can welcome them and somewhere in the conversation, mention that you have been praying for them. This can easily open the door to finding where they are spiritually.

Work Peers

Perhaps your greatest mission field, apart from your family, is your place of employment. You spend more hours at work than anywhere else. You know the persons who work with you. Pray for the right time to share the Good News with them from a heart of love and a life of service.

Our culture has taught us that religion is an individual/personal matter. We invade people's territory when we share our faith. We don't want to be rejected.

The devil will do all he can to discourage you from sharing your faith. Nearly every page of the New Testament reminds us that our faith is not readily accepted by the masses of people. We know the cross demands that we die to self and make Jesus Lord of our lives. We realize this is offensive to all who have not opened their lives to the Lord. Pray for the Holy Spirit to soften hearts to hear your testimony and be drawn to Jesus.

People You Already Know

People in your sphere of influence are numerous. Intentionally build a relationship with the banker, the postman, the mechanic, the barber or beautician, the doctor, the dentist, neighbors, school teachers, the crossing guards, bus drivers, and others.

Helen walked into the bank on Friday. She was greeted with, "Are you doing anything exciting this weekend?" She paused a moment and said, "I'm looking forward to worshiping God with my church family. It's the highlight of my week." Church is exciting when people are being transformed by the power of the Good News.

When I get my hair cut, I usually have a different beautician each time. To be congenial, they ask me what I do. Since I'm involved in ministry, this makes it easy for me to explore their beliefs about God and the church.

Since most people like to talk about their children or grandchildren, ask if they have a church family.

Acts of Service

The opportunities are endless: rake leaves, shovel snow or fix a board on a widow's porch. When someone is ill or in a car accident, take a meal or a plate of cookies. Offer to help with laundry or cleaning or whatever is needed. Don't feel you are a second class citizen because all you can do is "serve" people. When they thank you, share with them that God has been good to you. You are glad to pass on a bit of God's love. You may want to add, "He changed my life and made my life complete. I want you to know God loves you too."

In Matthew 25:35-36, Jesus lists six different categories of people that especially need his love: the hungry and thirsty, homeless, those sick and those in prison, as well as those who need a coat or blanket. Jesus said that we meet him every time we minister to a person in need.

Confront

There are occasions when you need to confront. If you have a good relationship with someone you know well, and he or she gets involved with using or selling drugs, an inappropriate sexual relationship or is into pornography, then you need to confront. If people respect you, they will hear you. If they do not respect you, there is little chance they will pay attention and may tell you to mind your own business. Regardless, the Holy Spirit can use your words later when they are more teachable.

Prayer Walks

Walk around your community stopping to pray in front of schools, churches, police and fire departments, hospitals, bars, courthouses and other public places. Our youth group includes many whose families have little or no interest in church. If appropriate, pray in front of those houses. Perhaps you will be invited inside, where you can thank the parents for permitting their child/youth to come to the youth group or church. Pray, asking God to bring his love and peace to all who go in and out their doors.

Restaurants

When the waiter or waitress serves your food, you might say, "Thank you. Do you have any prayer requests before we say grace?"

Special Days of the Year

Thanksgiving, Christmas and Easter are wide open doors for us to remind people of the importance of the Christian faith. When you meet anyone, including people you have never met, strike up a conversation by saying, "Thanksgiving is a great holiday. God has given us much to be thankful for." At Christmas time you might say, "It sure is a busy time of year. Are you ready for Christmas? Will you be able to celebrate Christmas in church?" Easter is the greatest day of the year. Before Easter, ask, "Will you be able to attend a church service on Easter?" After Easter, ask, "Were you able to attend the Easter celebration at church?" Allow the Holy Spirit to move you from speaking about church to Jesus.

Special Programs or Activities at Church

Create special programs such as Children's Sunday, Grandparents' Sunday, Back to School Sunday. Print attractive fliers and distribute them at work or at the Community Park or playground. Take time to talk with people as you distribute them.

Encourage your pastor to have something special for Friend Day, Children's Day, Mother's Day, Father's Day, Grandparents' Day; this makes it easier to invite unchurched people for these special days.

International Sunday

Most every community has international people. Learn to know them. Discover where they are in their relationship with Jesus. Some will know Jesus. Invite them to share their faith or to sing using their instruments, or find other ways to encourage them. They will encourage you and you will help to expand the vision and world-view of your church.

Spring, Summer or Fall Festivals

Children around your church need things to do. Invite them to an afternoon or evening of activities. Provide refreshments. Ask their parents to assist with the activities. Hopefully these contacts will begin to build a bridge to invite them to faith in Jesus.

Door-to-Door

As old fashioned as it is, going door-to-door is still an effective way to meet community people. I walk from house to house, handing out invitations to a special event at church, encouraging those who have a church and gently challenging those who don't go to church.

As I do this, I find myself spontaneously singing and praying as I walk. Going up and down porch steps is tiring for me, but my spirit is rejuvenated. This method may not be advisable in larger cities and apartment complexes.

Since false cults use this approach and go two by two, I often go alone which is less imposing. I enjoy chatting with people working on the lawn or sitting on the porch. Often children want to know if they can have a flyer. My wife Helen prays as I knock on doors. That makes all the difference.

Calling New Movers

When I was at Capital Christian Fellowship near Washington D.C., going house to house was not appropriate. The cliché was, "The only people who knock on doors are bill collectors."

For years, I made six hundred phone calls a month to new movers. This proved to be the most effective evangelistic tool in my fifty years of pastoral ministry. Hundreds of people were reached using this approach. For a minimal fee, "New Movers Evangelism" provides the names and phone numbers. I called these new movers and said in one breath: "Hello, I'm Pastor Dave from Capital Christian Fellowship in Lanham, if you have found a church family since you moved that is wonderful! If not, would you permit me to send a flyer inviting you to worship with us some Sunday?" One out of five gave an affirmative answer. Don't expect one call or flyer to bring them to church. I would call for six months and then say, "I don't want to waste your time or mine. I am going to take you off my list if that is okay." It was amazing how many wanted me to keep calling.

Today, many people have only cell phones instead of land lines, which makes it more difficult. If your church name is a denominational name, you will find it much more challenging to find new movers willing to visit your church.

Telemarketers

I often listen to telemarketers and end by saying, "Thank you for your call. You have a good day and God bless you." A friend of mine listens to their message and then says, "I listened to your message; I want to share a message with you." She then shares the Good News.

When someone calls, not realizing they have the wrong number, respond cheerfully and gives them God's blessings.

"God Bless You"

"God Bless You" is not a thoughtless, glibly spoken phrase. I try to always be smiling and especially pleasant as I pray for God to use these three words to remind people there is a God. Our culture is so secular that the vast majority of people never think of God. Those who have a close relationship with God often smile and respond with, "Thank you, and you too." Others, I can tell, are caught off guard and don't say anything. I pray at least they are reminded there is a God who wants to bless them.

At first when you do this, it may seem artificial or awkward, but ask God to give you a voice that comes from a heart of love, so that this simple, sincere phrase is one the Holy Spirit will use for God's glory.

Text Messages, iPhones, Facebook, etc.

Use modern media to share God's love. Even though this media is not as effective as face-to-face relationships, God can use it to advance his Kingdom. Paul writes that he is agonizing for those he has not met. (Col. 2:1). We can do the same as Paul.

Attractive Web Page

Most congregations have program designers who can keep their web page attractive and up to date. Persons who are considering checking out your church may find themselves checking first on your web site.

Coffeehouse Bible Study

For several years, I have been part of an interdenominational men's group that meets every Wednesday 7-8 a.m. at the local coffee shop. We always take a book of the Bible, usually a New Testament book, and read it several verses at a time. The discussion is quite animated. It has been one of the most energizing groups I have experienced. One reason the group is healthy is that we come from different backgrounds and denominations, Christians and unbelievers, with Jesus and his Holy Word as our unifying factor.

Because of the poor image of the church, it is best to have these studies at a neutral location rather than in a church building. Many people today who are turned off with "church" are not turned off with God. These groups become their church. I believe this will continue to be a wave of the future for making disciples who make disciples.

Taking a Personal Survey

If we are going to reach people, it's always interesting and helpful to know what people are thinking. I frequently approach people who I discern have time as they are sitting on a public bench, at a mall or park. I tell them I'm taking a survey of three simple questions. "What makes you happy?" "What makes you sad?" Most people will find it easy to answer these two questions. The final question is, "Does God have anything to do with what you shared with me?" This approach usually opens up further conversation for them to ask questions about God and faith.

For youth and younger adults, I have found it helpful to use the following approach: "I'm taking a survey. It only takes thirty seconds. Two questions: (1) "What do you think of Jesus?" (2) "What do you think of the church?" Most people have a positive image of Jesus but a negative image of the church. By now, you can tell if they are open to continuing the conversation.

After a short conversation, you may want to continue with the following questions adopted from "Dare 2 Share."

- Do you have a spiritual belief?
- To you, who is Jesus?
- Do you think there is a heaven and a hell?
- If you died now, where would you go?

Dare 2 Share

Dare 2 Share (www.dare2share) also uses the acrostic: **G-O-S-P-E-L** to help in sharing the Good News.

> **G**od created us to be with Him.
> **O**ur sins separate us from God.
> **S**ins cannot be removed by good deeds.
> **P**aying the price for sin, Jesus died and rose again.
> **E**veryone who trusts in Him alone has eternal life.
> **L**ife with Jesus starts now and lasts forever.

Serendipity

Wednesday as I pulled into the parking lot of the local library a woman came out the door staring at me. I was sure I didn't know her. She kept staring even as I parked my car. As I opened my door she walked toward me and said, "I am new in town, can you tell me where I can get help to prepare my income tax?" We talked and I said, "Do you have a church?" Standing in the parking lot we talked for 10-15 minutes. She came to church Sunday fifteen minutes early. Many people welcomed her. She enthusiastically entered into worship as the worship team lead us. Every Sunday we have a congregational noon meal which enables us to build relationship in a relaxed nonthreatening setting. She asked if I knew of a carpenter to hang mirrors. I went to her home, met her husband who had suffered a stroke, hung the mirrors, and dedicated their home. Together we experienced a powerful time of prayer. She is showing definite interest in small group Bible studies and the prayer team. As we walk with the Holy Spirit these serendipity occurrences encourage everyone.

The Guilt Approach Is Not Effective

If we present Jesus as the ticket to heaven, an escape from hell, and the seekers do not grasp a glimpse of the love of Jesus for themselves, they will go on living in defeat.

The guilt and death themes usually do not connect with people today, especially the younger generations. Since they don't believe in sin, they don't feel guilty, and many are not particularly interested in life after death. These themes are usually not a good starting point for a conversation about faith. But many feel lonely and alienated, and lack meaning in life. Introduce them to a life of purpose and satisfying relationships.

People receive Jesus because they believe he can do something for them. Don't forget to share how Jesus gives you joy, peace and purpose. You wouldn't think of trading those qualities for a meaningless life in the world.

In Summary

Jesus said, "I chose you and appointed you to go and bear fruit – fruit that will last." (Jn. 15:16). Loving people in your community means putting down deep roots and caring about those who live there. It goes against the "me first" mindset of our culture. Media continually tells us to "shop around" for the best deals, even if they are ten miles away. Get involved locally. Shop at the same stores. Eat at the same restaurants. Get to know the clerks by name and tip generously. Stand in the longest checkout line in order to greet the clerk you know. It will cost you a few minutes, but you are building relationships. You are a fisher of men and women – everyone is precious in God's sight.

The key is relational investments. People love being recognized and treated with dignity. It's amazing how much people will share if you slow down and listen. Go out of your way to learn the names and histories of the people you meet. Talk to the cashier and the people who assist you at the grocery store, bank, gas station, or post office. Don't scan your groceries in the self-serve line just to save time. Loving people is not always convenient. Touching lives for Jesus is exciting and has eternal benefits.

Jesus healed people and proclaimed the Good News. The early church declared the Good News as well as helping the widows and the poor. Loving words and actions must go together. The Holy Spirit will enable you to do more than you can ask or imagine.

Questions:

1. John Piper writes, "It is simple – not complicated at all. Tell people the good news of Christ from a heart of love and a life of service! That's it!" Discuss.
2. Which of the three dozen or more suggestions on how to open a conversation will you pray about and consider trying?

3. Most people love to talk about their pets, their children and the weather. Would you consider opening the conversation to a stranger and then mentioning God as suggested in this chapter? Why or why not?

4. Times of change and times of crisis usually make people more open to consider the need for faith. Whom do you know that is going through a difficult time that you can pray for and show deeds of kindness? Remember to ask if the person has a church family. If not, share Jesus and invite him or her to worship with you.

5. Can you see yourself using the "Dare 2 Share" approach, or the "Taking a Survey" approach? Why or why not?

6. Don't let a day pass without helping to remind people to be God conscious. Is that asking too much? You will discover a new joy and peace in your walk with Jesus.

7. Some people wear t-shirts that state openly and boldly their Christian faith. Is this something you might do? Why or why not?

8. What will it take to move you and/or your church to a new level of passion to share Christ?

9. Your prayer life will take on a new vibrancy if you are sharing Jesus on a regular basis. Discuss.

11

Good News and Discipleship

Make disciples of all ethnic groups. Matthew 28:18-20

Who is a Disciple?

Who is a disciple? Jesus had a way of making complicated things less complicated putting discipleship in terms a child can understand. Immediately following the institution of the Last Supper Jesus said, "A new commandment I give you: As I have loved you so you must love one another. By this everyone will know that you are my disciples, if you love one another." (John 13:34-35). These simple words have far reaching implications.

Paul sets forth fifteen characteristics of this love in I Corinthians 13 known as the love chapter of the Bible. Jesus clarifies in John 15:12-15, "My command is this: Love each other as I have loved you. Greater love has no one than this: to lay down one's life for one's friends. You are my friends if you do what I command. I no longer call you servants because a servant does not know his master's business. Instead I have called you friends, for everything that I learned from my Father I have made known to you." The primary characteristic of a disciple of Jesus is a person who is dominated by God's love and willing to give their time, energy, resources, even their life for others. For a disciple love is a verb.

Dan Miller a staff person for "DiscipleMakers: Reaching the campus... reaching the world," suggests that disciples must be faithful, available and teachable." Disciples must be dedicated to Jesus as Lord of their life. Is Jesus first? They must be available. They realize their time is not their own. They must be willing to relinquish their own desires and interests in the service of others. They want to help people make a difference. They are teachable, humble and really want to be taught so they can teach and disciple others who in turn make disciples. What percentage of church attenders in your congregation are disciples?

Where Do We Start?

Someone says, "Many people in our area don't attend church. We need to reach out more. But before we can reach out, we need to become better Christians. Many people in our church don't know what serious Bible study is let alone reading their Bible or giving a tithe."

Trying to make disciples apart from the Great Commission is impossible. Disciples share the Good News. It's part of their DNA – the focus of their lives. Can a person be a disciple if he or she never shares Jesus? Sharing the Good News is integral to making disciples. They go hand-in-hand.

Disciples are always moving people from nominal faith to genuine and real faith in Jesus. The most important way we make disciples is by modeling Jesus in all we do and say; this way people are drawn to the Savior. Paul says we are moving people from one degree of glory to another. (II Cor. 3:18). My wife Helen, in spite of her physical limitations, uses her gift of encouragement to move discouraged and struggling Christians to trust the Lord in the midst of their difficult circumstances or pain.

J. D. Moreland states, "Churches are producing 'empty selves' – people who don't reflect on their faith, members who value emotion and entertainment above serious Bible study and careful discipleship. Such churches are impotent to resist secular culture."[82] The American Church has failed miserably in making disciples.

Teach All Jesus' Commands

Not only did Jesus command us to make disciples, he instructs us to teach all his commands. Don't simply share the plan of Salvation thinking you have fulfilled your task. Teach new believers all that Jesus commands. (Matt. 28:20.) On the other hand, don't add to Jesus' teaching placing people in bondage, or pick and choose from his teaching sharing only the promises and neglecting the hard sayings of our Lord.

Paul says to the church at Ephesus, "I have not hesitated to proclaim to you the whole will of God." (Acts 20:27). The Amplified Bible reads, "I never shrank or kept back or fell short from declaring to you the whole purpose and plan and counsel of God." So many congregations go through the motions of "doing church" instead of experiencing believer's baptism, vibrant discipleship groups, and seeing lives transformed into the image of Jesus.

Jesus Set a High Standard

A man approached Jesus promising to follow him wherever he went. Jesus said, "Foxes have dens and birds have nests, but the Son of Man has no place to lay his head." (Lk. 9:58). Jesus invited another man to follow him, but the man wanted to first bury his father. More than likely the father was not ill but elderly. Jesus is saying, "Life is more important than death. Following Jesus and announcing God's Kingdom must take priority." A third man wanted to be a disciple of Jesus, but he thought he first had to get things straightened out at home and then he would follow him. Becoming a disciple of Jesus is first and foremost. God's work is something we must not put off. Seize the day! (Lk. 9:57-62).

Followers of Jesus are not guaranteed that even their basic need for shelter will be met. Can you imagine not going to your father's funeral? Life is urgent! Preach the Good News. Discipleship requires total devotion. Jesus may not literally ask us to live a homeless lifestyle, boycott the family funeral or leave without saying farewell. But a disciple must always to be ready to do whatever he asks. Jesus calls for radical obedience that will extend God's Kingdom.

Jesus also says that anyone who loves father, mother, son or daughter more than me is not worthy of me. Whoever does not take up his cross and follow me is not worthy of me. (Matt. 10:37-38). Family is very important but it must not be our idol.

We are the tools Jesus uses to redeem humanity, his servants to live and share the good news of redemption and make disciples. We can't obey Jesus' commands and at the same time build our own little kingdom. Jesus must be Lord. We are his instruments. Our passion must be to extend the reign of Christ, to love our neighbor as we love ourselves. Until those who call themselves Christian move to this level of commitment, our nation will continue down its moral slide.

Paul writes, "Do not offer (or present) the parts of your body to sin, as instruments of wickedness, but rather offer (or present) yourselves to God, as those who have been brought from death to life; and offer the parts of your body to him as instruments of righteousness." (Ro. 6:13). We are God's instruments!

There was a train wreck, and the bodies were strewn everywhere. The doctor on board was trying to help and do all he could, but he kept saying, "If only I had my instruments." Jesus is saying, "If only I had my instruments."

Discipleship Is Much More than Knowledge

Today when we think about making disciples, we think of a "perfect" curriculum. Paul reminds us that knowledge puffs up while love builds up. (I Cor. 8:1). Building relationships is paramount. To move infants to maturity in Christ, we cannot depend on a printed curriculum, no matter how good it is. Head knowledge must be integrated into our daily life.

Ninety percent of the forty or more times the word "knowledge" is used in the New Testament it translates the Greek root words, "gnosis or ginosko" which is experiential knowledge as compared to cognitive facts. Disciples are developed primarily through relationships rather than cognitive information although our foundation rests on the facts of God's Holy Word. Disciples must have a deep desire to truly know Christ as Paul says in Philippians 3:10 and Peter in II Peter 3:18).

Discipleship is mostly about how we live. Ideas, concepts and principles can be learned through books but lives can only be modeled with examples.

Jesus taught but he also shared his life. His disciples lived with Jesus. It was in that living that they began to understand what Jesus wanted to convey. For example, Jesus forgave sins. He did most of his ministry outside the temple. He touched the leper; spoke with a woman, even a Samaritan woman; he ate with sinners; he received children. His actions made a deeper impression than giving a lecture. Words can only go so far.

Jesus disciples copied this model. For example Barnabas modeled for Paul; Paul modeled for Timothy; Aquila and Priscilla modeled for Apollos. To be a disciple we must imitate our Master. Jesus' teachings are in the Bible, but we need to see Jesus in other people and allow their lives to impact us. To make disciples of Jesus we show with our lives what faith means in practical terms. Actions like forgiveness, kindness, love and peace are ones that impact other lives more than our words.

Converts or Disciples

Jesus commanded us to make disciples, rather than converts. While we don't base our theology on the number of occurrences of a particular word in the New Testament, the choice of words can give some indication of their importance. The word "Christian" appears three times, "convert" four times, "discipleship" two hundred seventy-five times, and "Lord" more than six hundred times.

Many times when people come to church they are simply asked if they want to become a member with little or no expectation of their becoming fully devoted followers of Jesus. Making disciples compels us to grow in our relationship to Jesus.

Why are Bible studies and prayer meetings so poorly attended? They are poorly attended because they become inward focused. When we witness daily, we will be challenged to pray for those we witness to, and to study God's Word so we can provide help to these persons who are searching for life and are being discipled. When they are in our midst, our prayer and Bible study become animated.

When people find new life in Jesus, they bring with them challenges that are only overcome by showing sacrificial love, faith-filled prayer, and relevant and meaningful Bible study. Bible studies and prayer times will not be vital over an extended period of time unless people are being won to Christ. "Babies" must be trained and that "forces" us to grow so we can nurture them. We must move from making converts to making disciples and train them to make disciples.

We have taken a truncated or abridged Gospel to many nations of the world. Our evangelists return with glowing numbers of those who are converted. In fact, it has happened that if you add their conversion figures together, you have more conversions than you have people. The great evangelist George Whitefield understood the difference between converts and disciples. When he was asked how many conversions he had, he replied, "I'll tell you six months from now."

Savior or Lord?

Many say, "Accept Jesus as your Savior," but do not mention that he must be our Lord. The New Testament nearly always puts Lord before Savior. If he is Lord, he will be our Savior. Multitudes think they are saved but have no concept or desire to make him Lord. Disciples of Jesus must make Jesus their Lord. If he is not Lord, we must ask if he is really our Savior.

Maturity Takes Time

You can't expect a four-year-old to have the maturity of a fourteen-year-old, or a twenty-year-old to have the maturity of a forty-year-old. People grow and mature over time at different rates. Progress isn't as linear as grade 1 and grade 2. We all know some twenty-year-olds who are more mature than some forty-year-olds.

Paul's admonition in I Corinthians 3:1-3 describes many of our churches today. "I could not address you as people who live by the Spirit but as people who are still worldly, - mere infants in Christ. I gave you milk, not solid food, for you were not yet ready for it. Indeed you are still not ready. You are still worldly." Hebrews 5:12 echoes the same concern: "By this time you ought to be teachers, and you need someone to teach you the elementary truths of God's word all over again. You need milk not solid food. Anyone who lives on milk, being still an infant, is not acquainted with the teaching about righteousness. But solid food is for the mature who by constant use have trained themselves to distinguish good from evil."

We must constantly ask, "Am I moving from milk to meat or am I still being spoon-fed baby formula?"

When Does Training Disciples Begin?

How long did Jesus make seekers wait before he sent them out to share the Good News? Jesus told the demon possessed man in the tombs who begged to go with him: "Go home to your own people and tell them how much the Lord has done for you, and how he has had mercy on you. So the man went away and began to tell in the Decapolis how much Jesus had done for him. And all the people were amazed." (Mark 5:19-20). In the ten cities of the Decapolis, not one city had less than 5000 people. Can you imagine the multitudes who were impressed with this man's testimony? Jesus began training him just as soon as he believed in him.

The woman at the well only met Jesus for perhaps an hour or two, but God enabled her to be an evangelist bringing many from her community to Christ. (John 4:41). Levi immediately held a banquet for his fellow tax collectors so he could introduce them to Jesus. (Matt. 9:9-13).

Jesus began discipling people before they fully understood what it meant to follow him. The 12 disciples still had questions and doubts after three years of traveling with Jesus and listening to his teaching, but Jesus used them from day one. We begin the training process as soon as there is a genuine spark of interest in exploring the Christian faith.

Build Faith Immediately

Just as soon as prebelievers show genuine interest, encourage them by telling them that God will use them to bring their friends, relatives and work peers to new life in Christ. I say to prebelievers, "You told me that you have relatives who are going through a divorce; another person you work with is living a life of sinful practices, another will soon be released from prison. God is going to use you to bring many of your friends and relatives to Christ. You will experience a greater joy than you ever imagined." It's important to build faith in persons who are showing sincere interest in Jesus even before they confess Jesus as Lord.

Peter's Model – II Peter 1:1-15

As Peter's life was coming to a close, he intentionally prepared believers to become disciples who would pass on their faith to the next generations. He gives us a helpful guide in moving people from infancy to maturity in Christ.

Here is the essence of Peter's outline in II Peter 1:3-14: God has given us everything we need to move from the elementary stage to maturity in Christ. He has given us many promises so that through these promises we can participate in his divine nature escaping the corruption in the world caused by evil desires. We do this by making every effort to add to our faith, God's goodness. Next develop knowledge, and then put your knowledge to work by exercising self-control – meaning we do what we know God wants us to do. Self-control will develop steadfastness, patience and endurance. The next level is purity and godlikeness, bringing every thought in line with Christ. Finally you love others and love God with a self-sacrificing love, the same love that Jesus expressed when he died on the cross.

Then Peter adds that if you keep growing in these qualities, they will keep you from being ineffective and unproductive. In fact, you will not stumble, and you will receive a rich welcome into the eternal kingdom of our Lord and Savior Jesus Christ. Following Peter's outline moves us from faith in Christ to loving others as Jesus loved and discipled us.

What Structure Can We Use to Make Disciples?

Jesus Is Our Model

Jesus called the disciples to be with him. (Mk. 3:14). He taught them in their context. Their relationship was more informal than structured. They observed his encounters with people. He welcomed sinners and eats with them. (Lk. 15:2). Jesus' teaching was more life-focused than cognitive information.

While we find it a challenge to take those being mentored with us as Jesus did, we need to meet regularly, with the agenda focusing on making Jesus' teaching active in our daily lives. We study the Scriptures and apply them to our context in our home, in our work and in our community.

Finding Mentors

Finding mentors is difficult. Most Christians don't see themselves as mentors. I have found that persons can attend church all their lives, but only a very few are willing to mentor a new follower of Jesus or mentor another Christian who desires to grow in his or her faith walk. Several reasons or excuses I hear: (1) I do not know Scripture well enough. (2) I have inconsistencies in my life so I am not qualified to disciple anyone. (3) I'm too busy, my schedule is full already. (4) I don't know how to disciple people; I'm afraid I can't fulfill their expectations. We must start with training persons to be mentors.

Finding Those Who Want To Be Mentored

Not only is finding mentors difficult, but it is just as difficult to find persons who want to be mentored. We have watered down Jesus' teaching to the point where most church attenders believe all you need to do to be a "good" Christian is go to church when it's convenient and give an occasional offering. In many churches, you can be an active member by giving verbal assent or embracing the church's doctrinal statement and its rituals and rules, without ever knowing Jesus. (Matt. 7:20-23).

Many youth and adults have gone through catechism without experiencing a life transformation that Jesus called being "born from above." They have not put off the old nature and clothed themselves with God's righteousness. There's little difference between them and the people of the world. They are good people but not godly people. The Great Commandment and the Great Commission are not the controlling and compelling passion of their lives.

One-On-One

I have been mentoring a business man for some time. We discuss how to make Christ central in his personal life, in his home relationship, in his business and in his recreation and community involvement. We discuss his Bible study and prayer life, his relationship with his wife and children, as well as employee relationships. I share my experience, my struggles, and we learn together. It's a joy to see him grow, as well as to experience growth myself.

Another unmarried couple with children came to church. We went through the plan of salvation, which they both claimed to have accepted. However, they did not give serious time to study any assignments. After several weeks, it became obvious that they were not willing to give effort to grow in their faith. We must pray for the Holy Spirit to give us eyes to see those who sincerely want to follow Christ, are willing to give him first place and are willing to be taught.

The Small Group Model

It's appropriate to meet one-on-one, but mentoring works better with two or three mentorees rather than one. Synergy occurs more naturally with two or three as compared to one-on-one. We rarely see Jesus interacting with individual disciples, but he frequently took Peter, James and John apart from the others. One-on-one often limits the quality of interchange. We are designed for community. We learn best in community.

Small groups with a passionate leader focused on discipling work well, as long as there is genuine love and honesty with both leader and mentorees. Unless the leader is mature, small groups often gravitate into social groups where you talk about everything but the challenges and struggles in walking in obedience to Christ in daily life. These groups often become Bible study groups with little accountability. The Christians experience little growth as they continue to live with sins of the spirit, such as jealousy, unforgiveness, anger and poor self image.

Mentoring a Larger Group

Jesus chose twelve. Sitting in rows in our church building has its limitations. It produces few disciples. Jesus worked with "circles." There was interchange between the teacher and the students. We are hard pressed to find lengthy sermons in the Bible. For the first three hundred years, the followers of Jesus did not have church buildings. They met in homes where interchange was natural. In this setting, disciples were developed, and the result was that they conquered the "mighty" Roman Empire.

In countries where Christianity is growing, the small group model predominates. Americans are so focused on numbers that we think the small group approach, as Jesus introduced, will not be effective. The opposite is true.

Can Disciples Be Made in Large Group Contexts?

Throughout church history, there have been times of great revival when nominal Christians became devoted followers of Jesus. When revival occurs, Christians are transparent with each other, confessing their sins and their lukewarmness. They earnestly pray for themselves and for those who do not know Jesus. They passionately share the Good News of Jesus. Disciples will continue to be made as long as there is transparency and accountability with each other and a passion to win people to our Lord.

Making Disciples in Mega-Churches

The largest church in the world, Yoido Full Gospel Church, in Seoul, South Korea, with 800,000 members has produced thousands of disciples. How do they do it? They have thousands of small groups scattered through the city and into the country.

The challenge is the same for all churches, regardless of size: to use the small group model as the most effective way to make disciples.

The Early Church – Acts 2:42-47

Perhaps the clearest Scripture setting forth the procedure or "formula" for making disciples is Acts 2:42-47. After Peter's message, people were cut to the heart, they repented and were baptized. How did this multitude of 3,000 become fully committed followers of Jesus? Verse 42, "They devoted themselves to the apostles' teaching and to fellowship, to the breaking of bread and to prayer." Verses 44-47, "Every day they continued to meet together in the temple courts. They broke bread in their homes and ate together with glad and sincere hearts, praising God and enjoying the favor of all the people. And the Lord added to their number daily those who were being saved."

These new Christians were taught by the Apostles and fellowshipped or spent time with each other on a daily basis. They ate together, prayed and worshiped together. Can you imagine being together on a daily basis, being taught God's Word, enjoying rich fellowship as you discuss and discern how this Word affected your daily life? They invited each other to their homes freely sharing their food. If anyone had a need, they shared what they had to meet the need. Healthy groups like these attract people to Christ.

Veteran Missionary Don Jacobs writes, "The early church met together on two levels – the house clusters and the larger area fellowships. Each had its own role. The house clusters provided for mutual sharing, while the area fellowships were a time for expounding the Word and for fellowship across cultural boundaries. These met the needs of Christians for mutual assistance, as well as to grow and evangelize."[83]

Accountability Is Key

Expose new Christians to the love of God in community where there is loving, solid accountability, and over time, many will grow to maturity in Christ-likeness. Why is this true? There is no accountability in larger groups. Some may argue that a dictator-hierarchy holds people accountable. A church dictator may hold people accountable, but a dictator does not give people the freedom to choose whether or not to follow Jesus. Dictators breed legalism. Jesus always gave people the choice to follow him or walk away.

One-Another Scriptures

Until we take the "one-another" exhortations of the New Testament seriously, there will be little discipleship. We must love one another, encourage one another, and admonish one another. Today in America, there is little desire for that level of accountability. Apart from accountability, we cannot make disciples. Love must be put into action or it is not love. Jesus said, "Love one another as I have loved you." Jesus took up his cross and we must do the same. (Matt. 16:24; Lk. 9:23).

In countries like China where disciples are trained in house churches, there is little need for church buildings and paid clergy. I believe the American church will be forced to move in this direction as persecution increases.

The Apprentice Model

It's been said, "Success without a successor is failure." Our churches are structured with many positions or offices such as teachers, deacons, elders, youth ministers, etc. If people in these positions are mature, the apprentice model can work well. However, the job description for these positions does not usually include the expectation that in order to hold a particular position or office, you must prepare your successor. Often it is difficult to find dedicated persons to take seriously their leadership role. Adding the responsibility of training a successor makes it even more challenging. However, there are mature disciples who do well using this model.

When I was a teen-ager, a mature Christian mentored me. He spent time encouraging me, answering my questions and teaching me so I could teach others. He made a difference in my life by helping to give me confidence to serve in a leadership position. He gradually stepped aside as he trained me to take his position.

Discipling Youth

Chet, our son, disciples thirty junior and high school youth. Many regularly participate in the Wednesday evening youth gathering. A number read their Bibles and witness their faith to their peers, even though they do not all come from Christian homes. One struggle is that those who neglect the Sunday worship do not feel a part of the larger church community. Consequently, when they graduate from high school, they graduate from church. Jesus designed the church to include all age groups. Unless the youth feel a vital part of the intergenerational community, they will not become mature disciples! To make disciples, we must make every effort to facilitate intergenerational relationships.

If you have a college age and young adult group in your congregation include the high school seniors in this group. This way when they graduate they will have peer connections and will hopefully participate in the life of your congregation.

The Household Principle

I have found one of the most effective approaches to reaching people and making disciples is the "household approach." The household principle is first mentioned in John 4:53. A government official came to Jesus requesting him to heal his son who was dying. Jesus told him to go, and his son would live. When the official realized his son's fever left at the time Jesus told him to go, he believed as well as his household. In Acts 10:24-48, Cornelius invited his relatives and a large number of friends to his house to hear Peter's message. They were all baptized.

In Acts 16:27-34, the jailer in Philippi who was guarding Paul and Silas was about to kill himself when he saw the doors of the jail open. But Paul shouted, "Don't harm yourself! We are all here." Paul and Silas preached the word to the jailer and his household. They believed and were baptized. In the same chapter (v. 15), Paul and his companions visited a prayer meeting on the beach. Lydia opened her heart to the Lord, and she and her household were baptized. In Acts 18:8, Crispus, the synagogue ruler, as well as his entire household, believed and were baptized.

This principle lends itself to making disciples since accountability is built into the household structure. I have been greatly blessed by using the household principle. It has brought scores of people to the Savior and helped to move them to maturity. At the beginning of a church plant, I sent letters to those on the streets close to where we began to meet and followed up with phone conversations. An unchurched father came to visit. The next Sunday he brought his wife and son. The son played an instrument and was eager to play for worship. I made sure the songs were appropriate. Next the son brought his wife, and soon other members of their family were coming. Over the next few years, more than two dozen persons came through that one individual. What an encouragement it was for me to welcome them into the body of Christ.

Persons of Peace

When Jesus sent the disciples in Matthew 10:9-11, his instructions were, "Do not take any gold or silver or copper to take with you... Whatever town or village you enter, search there for some worthy person and stay at their house until you leave." They were to find a person of peace; that is a person who is searching for peace, who would welcome them and become a beachhead for the Gospel in that area. Something in the person's response revealed the level of receptivity in his or her house. These persons are a bridge to others who will become disciples. Lydia, Levi, the Woman at the Well, and the Demoniac were persons of peace. Ask the Holy Spirit to help you identify people who have a deep desire to receive the Good News. With much prayer, the Holy Spirit will lead you to these persons in God's time.

What do persons of peace look like? (1) They receive the gospel freely. (2) They are respected and have a positive influence over their family, friends and those within their community. (3) They have the ability to effectively introduce church planters into their spheres of influence. (4) They bring and include others into the life of the church.

Some people are gatekeepers and herdsman. They have connections. They have discernment as to who may be open to receiving the Good News. Gatekeepers bring persons from various walks of life. Spotting these persons enables the Gospel to spread more rapidly.

When Helen and I moved to a new community, the congregation was ninety percent Caucasian, while the community was made up of more than fifty percent of African Americans and other nationalities. I contacted a "woman of color" with a small child. After some time she came. Over the next months, several families came because of her influence. She is a person of peace. When she brought new persons who knew Jesus, I made sure these "persons of color" were on the platform with me. Many nationalities came because they enjoyed worshiping in a church that was not segregated. Involving them and giving them visibility to the congregation sent the clear message that everyone was welcomed and needed in the body of Christ. God blessed our effort as we grew from 45 to 400.

Discipleship and Service

One study[84] reports that (1) Ninety-two percent of those surveyed said that service to others had a "positive effect" on their spiritual growth. (2) Service was as beneficial to them as other spiritual disciplines, including Bible study and prayer. (3) Eighty-eight percent of those who were serving were satisfied with their level of spiritual growth, while only forty-two percent of those who were not serving were satisfied with their spiritual growth. It's important to know that these service activities were mainly in the community, outside the four walls of the church. Service inside the church can easily become meaningless routine. We must get people out of church work and into the work of the church. Too often we are just doing laps and not making disciples.

The Social Gospel Does Not Make Disciples

Our son, Pastor Chet, spent eight months in one of the largest cities in America serving in a soup kitchen. Much of that time he was the "bouncer," forbidding men high on drugs from entering. His life was often in danger when he had to tell men they could not enter because of their behavior. He learned many things from that experience. The most important was that you can feed the hungry and shelter the homeless, spending untold time, effort and money, which usually result in only giving temporary relief. He came away from that experience convinced that Jesus is the only one who can change the heart and behavior of a person. Since then he has helped many find deliverance from drugs, alcohol and other fatal addictions, as they learn to trust Christ for deliverance.

Disciples Are the Aroma of Christ

We are the aroma of Christ to everyone. "God leads us from place to place in one perpetual victory parade. Through us, he brings knowledge of Christ. Everywhere we go, people breathe in the exquisite fragrance. Because of Christ, we give off a sweet scent rising to God, which is recognized by those on the way of salvation..." (II Cor. 2:14-15 Msg).

Others are not receptive to what is pure and good. They feel condemned in our presence. They resent us and joke about our beliefs. "Those on the way to destruction treat us more like the stench from a rotting corpse. This is a terrific responsibility. Is anyone competent to take it on? No—but at least we don't take God's Word, water it down, and then take it to the streets to sell it cheap. We stand in Christ's presence when we speak; God looks us in the face. We get what we say straight from God and say it as honestly as we can." (II Cor. 2:16-17 Msg).

In this sense, we witness to everyone as they observe our lives, our demeanor and our speech. Some have a positive response while others a negative one. After all Jesus said there is a time coming when "Everyone will hate you because of me." (Lk. 21:17).

We're in Christ's victorious parade as the world watches, in the procession of a conqueror, (Ro. 8:37), always led in triumph no matter how difficult life may be. It's because of Jesus that we give off a sweet scent.

Helen and I were on the way home from the rheumatologist. After having received a discouraging report, Helen said, "This did not catch God unawares. I just need to learn a new level of leaning on Jesus through pain." We stopped at the grocery store and the clerk said to Helen, "I like the fragrance you are wearing. What's it called?" Helen said, "I'm not wearing any fragrance. I'm allergic to perfumes." "Oh, but it's such a mild, pleasing scent." Helen surprised herself as she said, "Maybe it's the essence of Jesus." The clerk responded, "That would be a pleasant scent." The clerk, the bagger and Helen praised God together in a holy moment.

Disciples Are the Light of the World – Let It Shine

Jesus said, "You are the light of the world. A city on a hill cannot be hidden. Neither do people light a lamp and put it under a bowl, instead they put it on its stand and it gives light to everyone in the house. In the same way, let your light shine before men that they may see your good deeds and praise your Father in heaven." (Matt. 5:14-16).

We are the light and the salt of the earth, not we might be. Jesus said we are, so don't hide the light. We don't make it shine, we let it shine. Sometimes, followers of Jesus feel they cannot talk about how God is working in their daily lives for fear it will come across as boasting. But humbly "brag" about Jesus and the difference he makes in your life. (I Cor. 1:31).

I've been asked, "Don't you get tired of doing good?" When we do good works, people notice. I respond, "Sure I get tired but I enjoy helping people; it's rewarding and usually energizing."

Hebrews 6:10 reads, "God is not unjust; he will not forget your work and the love you have shown him as you have helped his people and continue to help them." "What is important is faith expressing itself in love." (Gal. 5:6).

You Are Jesus to People

Sharing Jesus and making disciples is a lifestyle; it's not something you turn off or on, it's what you do 24/7. When I walk into a store, I often pray, "Lord you live in me. Tell me what to say and do while I am here." It's thrilling, even electrifying, how God answers that prayer. You are Jesus to everyone. You are their Bible. That is not being arrogant or self-righteous. Trust Jesus to speak and live his life through you. As I keep saying, "More than 200 times, we are told in the New Testament that Jesus is in us and we are in him." We have the power of the resurrection in us. (Eph. 1:19). Yes, the supernatural becomes natural.

Richard Halverson, longtime Senate chaplain, prayed this benediction: "You go nowhere by accident. Wherever you go, God is sending you there. Wherever you are, God has put you there. He has a purpose in your being there. Christ, who indwells you, has something He wants to do through you wherever you are. Believe this, and go in His grace and love and power."

Questions:

1. Are you a mentor? Why or why not?
2. Disciples are always moving people from nominal faith to genuine faith in Jesus. The most important way we make disciples is by modeling Jesus in all we do and say; this way people are drawn to the Savior. How can you better model Jesus?
3. The most effective and challenging Scripture for making disciples is in Acts 2:42-47. What can you do to more fully live out this Scripture? What can your church do?
4. Of the different models for making disciples, which do you see yourself or your church incorporating effectively: (1) by being faithful to model Jesus in all we do and say, (2) by mentoring one-on-one, (3) by discipling via small groups, or (4) by apprenticing? Are there other ways we can make disciples?
5. Do you have a friend to whom you feel free to share? Do you believe your church or your small group is a safe place where you can share your heart and be held accountable?

6. Can you give examples of making disciples in your church, or in your small group?
7. Who in your context is a person of peace? Do all you can to encourage them.
8. What can you do to help youth who graduate from high school to stay connected to the church?
9. Do you see yourself as being Jesus to everyone you meet?
10. Richard Halverson's challenging benediction ends this chapter. Be sure to read it again. Can you sincerely pray this prayer?

12

Good News for Those on the Margins

When a church avoids ministering to people because of the pain and complications it may bring, that church is stunted and does not mature.

We need the poor and those in the margins of society more than they need us. We need to learn from each other. In Luke 4, Jesus stood up in the synagogue and read from Isaiah 61:1-2, "The Spirit of the Lord is on me, because he has anointed me to proclaim good news to the poor. He has sent me to proclaim freedom for the prisoners and recovery of sight for the blind, to set the oppressed free, to proclaim the year of the Lord's favor." In Matthew 11, John the Baptist is in prison questioning if Jesus is truly the Messiah. Jesus tells John's disciples to tell John, "The Good News is being proclaimed to the poor."

James writes, "God has chosen those who are poor in the eyes of the world to be rich in faith and to inherit the kingdom he promised those who love him." (Jas. 2:5).

Emergency Room Ministry

Why Have We Neglected Those on the Margins?

While everyone is a potential ministry focus, God has a special place for those on the margins. Everyone needs to have a heart for hurting people! There are nearly 400 Scripture passages demonstrating God's concern for orphans, widows, prisoners, immigrants, homeless, the poor, the hungry, disabled, and sick. "This is the sin of your sister Sodom: She and her daughters were arrogant, overfed and unconcerned; they did not help the poor and needy." (Eze. 16:49). Also according to *The Poverty and Justice Bible*, there are almost two thousand verses in Scripture that deal with poverty and justice.

Whom do you know who is on the margins? Shane Claiborne asked a group of persons who claimed to be strong "followers of Jesus" whether Jesus spent time with the poor. Nearly 80 percent said yes. Then he asked whether they spent time with the poor, and less that 2 percent said they did. He writes: "We can admire and worship Jesus without doing what he did. We can applaud what he preached and stood for without caring about the same things. We can adore his cross without taking up ours... The great tragedy in the church is not that rich Christians do not care about the poor but that rich Christians do not know the poor.... When the rich meet the poor we will see poverty come to an end." (*The Irresistible Revolution*, pp.113-114.) Most Christians in American do not have an in-depth relationship with anyone on the margins. We tend to isolate ourselves from not only the billions of poor in our world but from the poor in our own communities and cities. Multitudes on the margins are left behind, as the more affluent move to the suburbs.

Why Does this Occur? The Curse of the Car

No, I'm not suggesting we drive a horse and buggy. How has the car been a curse? We are constantly striving to move up the economic ladder of success. As soon as we receive a pay increase, we think of updating our wardrobe, a better car, purchasing or moving to a new house or better location. Do we move because there are no people where we are presently? There are many more people in the lower income sections of our towns and cities per square mile than in upscale suburbia. We move to have better schools, or to separate ourselves from the congestion, crime and poverty in the poorer sections of town. In doing this, we cut ourselves off from those Jesus said we are to invite to his heavenly banquet. (Lk. 14:21-24).

Before there were cars, the poor and the more economically sufficient people lived side by side. In New Testament times, the poor lived beside the rich. The slaves were often the doctors and the managers of households. Many of them were middle class people. Many other slaves were poor. Widows and beggars were common. They lived in close proximity to the more well-to-do.

The church in Philippi was the most joyful of the New Testament churches. Might this be true in part because of the way this church began: Lydia, its first member, was a wealthy foreign woman, while the second member was a formerly possessed, fortune-telling slave girl at the bottom of the social scale. The third was a common laborer, a jailer posted to guard the town's prison together with his family. (Ac. 16).

God's grace is for all persons, those on the margins as well as those in the main stream of society. It's my personal experience, as well as observing many congregations as a church consultant, that there is a special joy and a greater moving of God's Spirit found in congregations where there is a variety of cultures and persons of economic strata. Homogeneous congregations are often ingrown and provincial.

If many of our churches in America would have stayed in the inner city rather than moved to suburbia, our churches would be lighthouses in places where the streets are now full of crime.

Lance Ford writes that:

> We don't take these passages (concerning the poor) seriously. "I can't open my home up to that lady and her two toddlers. I know she has no place to live and I have a space bedroom, but that's just not practical for me as this time in my life." Individualism and desire for comfort and privacy chokes out the Word and our missional imagination along with it, nullifying our effectiveness as agents of the kingdom of God. Vince Miller wrote about the shutting down of our imagination due to our fixation with the American Dream: [85]

> Two generations ago, it was not uncommon for families to raise five or more children in two-or three-room houses. Our inability to image how this was possible is a testament to the psychological skills we have lost. Now it is a common expectation that each child should have her or his own room. This arrangement requires an enormous amount of resources and renders us less able to share our dwellings with others in hospitality... Maintaining a family in this system make it unlikely that other people's needs will ever present themselves. If and when we do encounter them, we are likely to be so preoccupied with the task of maintaining our immediate families that we will have little time and resources to offer. The geography of the single-family home makes it very likely that we will care more about the feeding of our pets than about the millions of children who go to bed hungry around us. [86]

Lance Ford continues: Currently the average American family lives in a home that is over three times the size of the average American house from the 1950s. This is despite the fact that family units are smaller now... Another sign of overt consumption is evidence by the data regarding the self-storage business. It is a twenty-three billion dollar industry that rakes in more than the entire entertainment industry.

"Prosperity Gospel"?

There is an imbalance in much preaching today which overemphasizes God's promises of material blessings. While God blesses us materially, multitudes of poor die who are sincere followers of Jesus. Jesus was a refugee. (Matt. 2:13-15). He had no place to lay his head. (Lk.9:58). He said, "Life does not consist in an abundance of possessions." (Lk.12:14). Jesus did not die to make us rich in this world's goods. (II Cor. 8:9). Paul understood this when he wrote, "We are poor but make many rich." (II Cor. 6:10).

"It is a great principle with George Muller that it does not become the children of God to be ostentatious in style, appointment, dress, or manner of living. He believes that expensiveness and luxury are not seemly in those who are the professed disciples of the meek and lowly One who had no place to lay his head."[87]

Jesus Identified and Spent Quality Time with the Misfits in Society

Jesus said in Luke 14:12-14 that we are not to invite our families or anyone who can invite us back like our rich neighbors, but rather to invite those we know who cannot return the invitation. The people understood clearly what he was saying, because persons on the margins surrounded them. He said to invite the poor, the crippled, the lame and the blind. We must have a heart for those on the margins. The idol of many American families is their family, church is pushed somewhere down the ladder. Why are we afraid of strangers even though Jesus makes it clear it is our responsibility to reach out to them?

In Matthew 22:10, Jesus in another parable told the servants to go out into the streets and gather all the people they could find, both good and bad, until the wedding hall was filled with guests. The Greek word for "bad" appears 25 times in Matthew. This is the only time it is translated "bad" in the King James Version. Sixteen times it is translated "evil" and eight times "wicked." Most modern versions use evil. Jesus makes it clear that he wants us to seek "evil or wicked" people as well as "good" people.

"The tax collectors and sinners were all gathered around to hear him... The Pharisees and the teachers of the law muttered, 'This man welcomes sinners and eats with them.'" (Lk. 15:1). Again they said, "Here is a glutton and a drunkard, a friend of tax collectors and sinners." (Matt. 11:19).

Following is a quote from Shane Claiborne's book, *The Irresistible Revolution*, p. 127
Jesus did not seek out the rich and powerful in order to trickle down his kingdom. Rather he joined those at the bottom, the outcasts and undesirables, and everyone was attracted to his love for people on the margins. (We know that we all are poor and lonely anyway, don't we?) Then he invited everyone into a journey of downward mobility to become the least... As Sister Margaret, puts it, "We are trying to shout the gospel with our lives." Many spiritual seekers have not been able to hear the words of Christians because the lives of Christian have been making so much horrible noise. It can be hard to hear the gentle whisper of the Spirit amid the noise of Christendom."

Those in Prison

There are two million prisoners in the United States; that's more than any other country in our world. There is at least another million in the parole system. Jesus said we are to visit those in prison. Prisoners, like the poor, are often more open to the Good News than those who are living outside prison walls. Jesus said that he came not to call the righteous but sinners. If we obey Jesus' command, our churches will be messy. Most Christians don't like messy churches.

Do we want "bad," "evil," or "wicked" people to come into our lives and into our churches? That's who Jesus said we are to invite as well as those who we believe are "good." I see "good" people as the volunteer firemen, ambulance personnel, school teachers, coaches, librarians, community workers, volunteers, etc. They need Jesus just as much as those who are evil. But most people, including Christians, do not believe that. They think because they are "good," they will be ushered into heaven. There is a huge gap between being good and being godly. If being good ushered you into heaven, Jesus died in vain.

Luther in the 16th Century made it clear that salvation is not by works but by "grace through faith." Paul complimented all the other churches except the Galatian Church. Why? The Galatian Christians were replacing faith in Christ with good works. It appears the self-righteous spirit of the Galatians was a more momentous sin than the carnality and wickedness in the Corinthian church.

In the parable of the great banquet, Luke 14:15-24, the master sent his servants to invite the guests but they all made excuses: one just got married, another bought real estate, and yet another purchased farm equipment. The master was angry and told the servants to bring in the poor, the crippled, the blind and the lame, but there was still room. The master said, "Go out to the road and country lanes and make them come in, so that my house will be full. I tell you, not one of those men who were invited will get a taste of my banquet."

The Greek word for "make them come" appears only seven times in the New Testament. It conveys the idea that there is no option – it is something that must be done. I checked nineteen translations and six say, "make them come"; six say "compel"; four employ the word "urge"; two use the word "force"; and one says, "drag them in." We must urge, make or compel people to come to the heavenly banquet! How do we do that? How did Jesus do it? He gave his life and we must do no less. (Matt. 10:38).

Paul Identified with the Misfits

When Paul and Barnabas went to Lystra, they healed a man who was born lame. (Ac.14:8-10). In Philippi, Paul cast out the evil spirit in a female slave. (Ac. 16:16-18). In Acts 19:11-12 we read, "God did extraordinary miracles through Paul, so that even handkerchiefs and aprons that had touched him were taken to the sick, and their illnesses were cured and the evil spirits left them."

In Corinth, Paul identifies the "misfits" as persons who were immoral as compared to those in poverty and those in need of physical healing. He warns that we are not to be deceived: "Neither the sexually immoral, nor idolaters, nor adulterers, nor men who have sex with men nor thieves nor the greedy nor drunkards nor slanders nor swindlers will inherit the kingdom of God. And that is what some of you were. But you were washed, you were sanctified, you were justified in the name of the Lord Jesus Christ." (I Cor. 6:9-11).

Many Prominent Persons in the Bible Were Moral Misfits

Cain, Moses, David and Paul were all murderers. Aaron, the first high priest, led the people astray with the making of the golden calf. Noah got drunk, and Peter denied Christ. Does your church have a culture that allows for authentic openness about messy lives? The church is a motley crew. Eugene Peterson has observed that the church is composed of equal parts of mystery and mess.

The Church Should Be Like a Hospital Emergency Room

I spent several hours in an emergency room the other week where people were coughing, crying, and one collapsed on the floor. It was not a pretty scene. Working with people on the margins, you may find yourself cleaning up vomit, dealing with bugs and smells of all kinds.

When you hug a smelly person, you will pick up their scent, but they will also pick up the fragrance of Jesus from you. It gets messy working on the margins. One father who lost his infant child was so drunk at the cemetery that we had to hold him up so he didn't fall into the open grave. Almost every day, I relate to a man in his fifties who has come off alcohol and drugs. Money burns a hole in his pocket. He can't control his appetite for nicotine, junk food or eating in a restaurant. In spite of this, it's encouraging to see him grow in faith. The past few months, he gives me money toward his tithe and other necessities, so he doesn't spend it at the beginning of the month.

Reaching Those on the Margins Is Not Easy

Invading the devil's territory is never easy. Reaching those on the margins is tiring spiritually, emotionally, mentally and physically. (I Thess. 3:5; Gal. 4:11). Paul says he became all things to all people to win them to Christ. (I Cor. 9:22). This requires sacrifice. Actions speak louder than words – this is especially true for those on the margins. They have been hurt. Only love in action will impact their life. There is no expansion of God's Kingdom without costly sacrificial service. It's been said that the church is where the person you least want to live with lives. If we are to obey the Great Commandment and the Great Commission, we have no choice but to minister God's love to everyone.

Compassion means to "suffer with." Whatever the capacity for human suffering, the church has a greater capacity for healing and wholeness. There is no sinful situation that God's resurrection power can't conquer.

To some weary Christians in the immoral context of Corinth, Paul writes, "Always give yourselves fully to the work of the Lord, because you know that your labor in the Lord is not in vain." (I Cor. 15:58). The needs are overwhelming and victory for many is often slow. Paul writes, "Encourage the disheartened, help the weak, be patient with everyone." (I Thess. 5:14).

"The controlling factor is not the needs of the people but the command of Jesus. Intimacy with Jesus is the key! The danger is that God's call will be replaced by the needs of the people, and sympathy will overwhelm the meaning of being sent by Jesus. The needs are so enormous that every power of the mind falters and fails. We forget that the reason we serve is not primarily the elevation of the people, their education, nor their needs, but first and foremost the command of Jesus."[88]

Serving without having an intimate relationship with Jesus will dry you up. Jesus reminded Martha that Mary has chosen the one thing that is needed. (Lk. 10:42). We will burn out working *for* Jesus, but if we work *with* Jesus, we will live in the refreshing power of his Holy Spirit. Our service must come from a heart of love. We must take time to sit at the feet of Jesus like Mary rather than serve with sweat and human effort.

The past few days at LifeBridge Community Church, we helped a homeless person and a person with bed bugs, installed a stove for a family lacking heat, distributed food to needy families, provided transportation for others, and taught Spanish and English classes. We frequently help people move. There are calls for funds for gasoline and to help pay rent and utility bills.

The majority of Sundays in my fifty years of pastoral ministry, I provided transportation for people who had no other way to church. This was true even in some middle income towns. Those on the margins are mostly everywhere, if we have eyes to see them and hearts to love them.

In our community, there are few places open for people to congregate after 6 p.m., except at the bars. In our new addition at LifeBridge, we are planning to open a coffee shop where persons can come to a wholesome atmosphere after the usual working hours. A top quality thrift store is also part of our building expansion to assist persons by providing clothing of good quality at a fair price.

Fishing for People Is Messy Business

Jesus went where there was a need. Fishermen know that the convenient time is usually not the best time to catch fish. It takes long hours of hard work because fish don't jump into the boat. We must fish for them.

"Sometimes we want to help people without getting too close to them. But to show and model love, we have to get close to those we serve, even when it isn't comfortable or clean."[89] "Imagine Jesus going out into towns and villages during his public ministry and proclaiming his Gospel without accompanying acts of healing and helping. (Matt. 9:35). Do we really think our Lord would have gained a hearing, much less a following, or established the credibility of his message—without displaying some proof that his Gospel was real? Why would we ignore such a model?"[90]

A Special Challenge for Small Churches

My experience is that often emotionally unstable people are drawn to small churches, because this is where they find love and acceptance. Some, not deliberately, but because they are so starved for attention, absorb the energy of everyone especially the leaders. The unstable church members may become frustrated and walk away from church. Leaders need the Holy Spirit's wisdom and tough love, using Christ-like gentleness and firmness, to minister effectively with these people.

Large Churches

According to the Hartford research, the largest churches attract a fairly well-defined demographic. The average age of a mega church attendee is 40. Nearly a third of them are single and, on the whole, the mega church crowd is more educated and wealthier than the average members of smaller churches. In terms of distribution, there tends to be more mega churches in suburban rather than in urban or rural areas.

But which churches are reaching the people who fall outside this demographic and location? Small churches... Smaller churches can reach the people on the margins who often are not attracted to larger congregations...

Congregations of between 30 and 300 people... converge the best features of a small and a large church. They provide the critical mass necessary to remain energetic about mission, but they are intimate enough to be conducive to authentic community... Smaller, nimbler congregations are the only way to reach the margins... [91]

The Harvest Is Plentiful

Jesus said the harvest is plentiful. (Matt. 9:37). But there is a problem, there are too few workers. The first thing Jesus told the disciples to do was pray. Our natural response is usually not first to pray, but instead get busy and try to correct the problem. Jesus said that the focus of our prayers is to send workers to reach the multitudes who are harassed and helpless, rather than focus on the problem. Why is this? Jesus knew the basic problem is the church. We are reluctant to get our hands dirty. If we are going to make an impact in our world, we must be mobile. We must move outside our comfort zone and enter the field to find the good soil and be his harvesters. The government can feed the hungry, provide shelter, and medical help but the government cannot build relationships. That's our job as workers.

In the Roman world, unwanted babies were placed on the door steps and left to die. The Christians came and rescued the unwanted children, showing them love and caring for them. If every church in the United States would take in one needy child, the poverty and crime of our nation would be greatly reduced.

Bob spent every spare minute at the bar. He was living with his girl friend and her children. I visited them several times. They started coming to church, accepted Christ and decided to be married. Bob knew his friends would not come to a church wedding, so he asked me to marry them in the bar. I had the privilege of presenting the Good News to those in the bar who wouldn't darken the door of the church. Bob went back to the bar many times, not to drink but to share what God was teaching him.

Seek the Lost

Can you imagine Jesus building a fence to keep the neighbors away? Jesus came to seek and save lost people. (Lk. 19:10). Jesus searched for, he intentionally looked for lost people who would follow him. He had to go through Samaria because the Holy Spirit wanted him to reach the despised Samaritans. (Jn. 4:4). He looked for Zacchaeus in the tree. (Lk. 19:5). He called the twelve disciples and chose the seventy-two evangelists. Jesus leaves the ninety-nine and seeks the lost sheep. (Lk. 15:3-7). He was intentional in his outreach. In Luke 10 he reminds us to seek the person of peace. Who are you seeking?

We must be intentional. Like Jesus, we seek people who are hungry for meaning. Many people don't believe they are lost. They see themselves as basically good people who have bought into the philosophy, "I'm okay, you're okay, everyone is okay." They believe we will all go to heaven, if there is such a place. Jesus came not to call the righteous or those who think they are "good enough" but sinners. (Matt. 9:13).

Those on the margins are often more receptive to the Good News because of their need for love and acceptance. "The god of this age has blinded the minds of unbelievers, so that they cannot see the light of the gospel of the glory of Christ, who is the image of God." (II Cor. 4:4). Sometimes people say, "I found God." It's more accurate to say, "God found me." We are called to witness Jesus' presence in the world. He's already there but people are blind to his presence. Ask the Holy Spirit to guide you to the open and receptive hearts, to the good soil that will produce disciples.

A woman told me, "I've been praying and witnessing to my neighbor for twenty years. She does not seem to be one step closer to God." She described her friend as having a lucrative job, excellent health and a nice house. Two suggestions: first, pray for God to bring into her life whatever it takes to wake her up. That sounds cruel, but wouldn't we rather see her suffer for a few years than spend eternity in hell? Secondly, perhaps you need to "shake the dust off your feet" and seek others who are more receptive. (Lk. 10:11). There are multitudes all around you who need Jesus.

Lost Sheep and Lost Son

In Luke 15, Jesus goes after the lost sheep but not the lost son. Why? The lost son had not come to the end of himself. There are times when we should not post bail for the prodigals because their hard hearts are not yet broken. As soon as there is repentance, we see the Father reach out. He welcomes the lost son with a festival of celebration. The Holy Spirit will give you the wisdom to tell the difference between the lost sheep and the lost son.

I received a call from a young man. He is living with his girl friend, the mother of his second child. He wanted money because his car stopped running. He has difficulty holding a job and makes poor financial decisions. He has not learned responsibility since family and friends come to his aid. In these situations, we need to show tough love like Jesus did with the prodigal.

You Can Cause a Party in Heaven

In Luke 15, the scripture depicting the lost coin, the lost sheep and the lost son, we find the only place in the Bible where we are told we can cause a party in heaven. I'm sure heaven enjoys seeing God's people praise, worship and serve him, but it's obvious that heaven sees lost people coming to Jesus as a reason to celebrate.

As you walk in obedience to the Holy Spirit, he will lay individuals on your heart. Those are the ones you seek. Jesus saw the crowds, but he could spot persons who would be receptive. Ask God to give you his perception. As you pray and tune into the Holy Spirit, there will be times when you know the thoughts or the hearts of those you witness to. It's the gift of discernment. (I Cor. 12:10; Mark 2:8).

Sacrifice

Thousands die each year for sharing the Good News. After Jesus told about those who were killed when the tower fell on them and those who were slaughtered at the temple, (Lk. 13:1-3), he says, "Unless we repent we too will perish." Then he continues, "A man had a fig tree planted in his vineyard, and he went to look for fruit on it, but did not find any. So he said to the man who took care of the vineyard, 'For three years now I've been coming to look for fruit on this fig tree and haven't found any. Cut it down! Why should it use up the soil?' 'Sir,' the man replied, 'Leave it alone for one more year, and I'll dig around it and fertilize it. If it bears fruit next year, fine! If not, then I'll cut it down.'"

We wouldn't extend mercy to a plant that occupies garden space for three years unless it is productive, but God's mercy goes beyond ours. However, he too says at some point, "Cut it down." Our job is to live a life of repentance and faith and to call others to do the same.

Let's be conscious of those on the margins who need hope and eternal life. But be aware that the "good" people you rub shoulders with every day will perish, if you do not fulfill your responsibility to build relationships with them and share the Good News.

We Need Gagging Christians

In Acts 10 and 11, God let the sheet down from heaven three times to teach Peter to call no man unclean if God accepted him. I believe Peter wanted to gag when he saw the reptiles in that sheet. We need more "gagging" Christians who, like Peter, learn that God wants to stretch us so we can experience the joy of seeing people of different nationalities, cultures and economic status come into our lives and into our churches. This is a tremendous challenge for most traditional congregations composed of homogeneous ethnic families.

Paul says that we were gentle among you – like a mother caring for her little children – we shared our lives with you. We love, we listen, and we care and give our time. We learn God does not show favoritism but accepts people from every nation who reverence him and do what is right. (I Thess. 2:7-8).

Rewards Will Come

When you pray and work diligently with an unchurched family and they finally walk through the door, your worship is energized. This is especially true for the people who invited them and poured their lives into them. As a pastor, your message is animated. The singing bounces off the wall. There is a new level of joy. Your faith is increased and your zeal is contagious. A lost sheep is on the way to coming home and you celebrate! Heaven joins in your celebration.

Questions

1. Do you know people by name who are on the margins? Describe their condition. How can you build a relationship with them? Are you comfortable being with them?
2. Jesus said we are to invite those who cannot return the invitation. (Lk. 10:14-16). How will you obey Jesus' teaching? When Thanksgiving Day comes instead of taking them a meal invite them to sit around your table.

3. Is your church a welcoming and assimilating community for those on the margins? If not, what will it take for this necessary change?

4. Do you have a program to regularly assist those who are living in poverty, or who are disabled or sick?

5. Do you know anyone in prison? Have you gone to visit him or her?

6. More than fifty percent of residents in nursing homes never receive a visit. Would you and/or your church go to relate to them? Perhaps take a group to sing and share a worship service together.

7. At no time in the history of our world have there been more people living in poverty. One billion live on less than one dollar a day. Are you praying for these people and helping by giving to Christian relief efforts? What more can you and your church do to help these people?

8. Discuss the statement, "We will burnout working for Jesus but working with Jesus will energize us."

9. Explain how the "American Dream" contrasts with Jesus' Kingdom. See Matt. 6:33, Lk. 9:23 and Heb. 10:34.

13

A Welcoming and Assimilating Community

The Great Commission Demands We Love Jesus as well as His Church

Love Your Church

Today, many Christians claim they love God, but they have little respect for his church. Some criticize, complain and speak negatively about the church because they have been hurt. Christ died for his church. You cannot be a welcoming community without a love for your church. Furthermore we are commanded not to neglect to meet together, especially as we see the Day of Christ approaching. (Heb. 10:25).

When the church is passionate about the Great Commission, a strong community will develop. As a church focuses outwardly it becomes a healthy church internally. When Christians proclaim the Good News to their community, the glue of the church community will hold the members more tightly to each other because a common vision unites God's people.

A Welcoming Community Must Become an Assimilating Community

Assimilation is the process used to encourage first-timers to continue coming until they accept Jesus as their Lord and Savior, commit themselves to the local church, and become disciples who make disciples. We assimilate people by loving them and meeting a need in their lives. Their need is the door for God to use you to bring them to Jesus and to build a nurturing relationship with them.

To be an assimilating community, the church must create opportunities for people to grow in relationship with Jesus and with each other. The church needs to welcome people as they are. The church is a community of grace not grades. In this atmosphere of love and grace, lives will be transformed by Christ. Jesus made it clear that showing love for one another is the key for making our discipleship obvious and effective. (Jh. 13:34-35).

A church will reach as many as it has the capacity to love. Love people until they ask "why." Love like Jesus or better yet, allow Jesus to infuse your very nature with love.

The early church in Acts 2 loved, supported and depended on one another. There were no needy people among them, because they shared what they had to meet the needs of all. They met daily for prayer, fellowship, studying the Scripture and sharing meals together. Can you imagine how your church would change if you met daily? When revival sweeps across a nation, Christians meet frequently to encourage and build up Christ's Body.

Many times throughout the New Testament Christians address each other as "brother" or "sister." While we may not feel comfortable with this nomenclature it indicates the closeness we need to cultivate as God's children born into God eternal family.

Few if any lives will be transformed from darkness to light without a supportive community. It's nearly impossible to overcome evil addictive habits without the support of brothers and sisters. Galatians 6:2, "Carry each other's burdens, and in this way you will fulfill the law of Christ." Romans 15:1, "We who are strong ought to bear with the failings of the weak." Genuine New Testament community can never be practiced alongside the American lifestyle of individualism.

The New Testament sets forth seventeen ways we are to love one another.
- belong one to another, Ro. 13:5
- be devoted one to another, Ro. 2:10
- honor one another, Ro. 12:10
- welcome one another, Ro. 14:1
- be of the same mind, Ro. 15:5
- accept one another, Ro. 15:7
- admonish one another, Ro. 15:14
- greet one another, Ro. 16:3-6, 16
- serve one another, Gal. 5:13
- bear one another's burdens, Gal. 6:2, 10

- bear with one another, Eph. 4:2
- submit one to another, Eph. 5:21
- encourage one another, I Thess. 5:11
- pray for one another, Jas. 5:16
- teach and counsel one another, Col. 3:16

We cannot make disciples unless we take these "one-another" Scriptures seriously putting them into practice. Most churches receive a very low grade when they evaluate themselves by these "one-another" commands. Too often we are self-centered: "I'll do as I please. I'll take care of my business and you take care of yours."

The church in America will never be strong until we experience true community which includes loving accountability. People who simply warm the pew often become critical. As the Holy Spirit directs you it is possible to turn some of these critical spirited people around if you get them involved on your team to help impact your community for Christ.

Being Friendly or Being a Friend

There are a million miles between being friendly and being a friend. Every church says they're a friendly church. Being a friend demands sacrifice. Building friendships affects your schedule, your social life, your wallet, and your lifestyle. Simply being friendly will not reach people who will stay and be discipled. Being a friend will. To repeat, people are not looking for a friendly church as much as they are looking for friends.

When you go to a ball game or community concert, golfing, shopping, or eating out, invite seekers to go with you; or have them over for a backyard cookout. Invite some of your church friends for them to meet. It's obvious, but it must be said, you will need to be intentional or you'll soon allow the Great Commission to fade, because it involves sacrifice on your part. Jesus was intentional to leave heaven to rescue us.

Everyone Needs Significance, Community and Transcendence

We all, Christians and non-Christians, need significance, community and transcendence. Keeping these three things in mind will be helpful in assimilating people so they become disciples who make disciples.

Significance

Jesus was a master at helping people to feel significant. He asked questions and he asked people to help him. They felt respected. He gave them significance. He asked the woman at the well for a drink of water. When he raised Lazarus from the dead, Jesus asked the people to unwrap him. He used the little boy's five loaves and two fish to feed the multitude. He honored Mary and Martha by going to their home for a meal. He frequently asked those who came for healing what they wanted him to do, even though their needs seemed obvious. Jesus made people feel significant.

When we ask non-threatening questions, we give people the platform. We listen. People don't care how much we know until they know we care. People can't hear until they have been heard. Give them your undivided attention. All people, no matter what their jobs or their circumstances, can teach us something if we are willing to learn from them. Conversation not lectures indicates we respect them as persons.

Asking people to help you as Jesus did gives them significance. When prebelievers begin to come to church, what might we give them to do? They could hand out the weekly programs, play on the church sports team, perhaps play an instrument in the worship band, bring food for refreshments or for the carry-in-meal, set or put away tables and chairs. They may enjoy going on a service project with you. Inviting them in a loving, nonthreatening way to your small group or any church activity will also make them feel they are wanted and included.

As long as new people are not given any real responsibility, they will approach church with a consumerist mentality. Attenders who make a weekly habit of coming, sitting through the worship service and then leaving until the next Sunday often fall into a dangerous, selfish "what's the church doing for me" mindset. They are takers, and takers become spoiled. When seekers offer suggestions affecting the life of the church, too often bureaucracy stymies conversation and they feel rejected.

Community

There are two things you cannot do alone: get married and be a Christian. Someone said, "I need another sinner like myself; perhaps together we can keep each other accountable and on the path of life." We need each other. Solitary confinement is assigned to those needing to be severely punished. Adam needed a help mate. God created humankind to have fellowship.

God wants our fellowship.

Why do bars thrive? Bars prosper because people need community. Too often people feel condemned when they are around Christians. (Matt. 7:1-5). People must feel love and acceptance when they meet you and your Christian friends.

Unless people find a supportive relationship when they start to explore faith, they will quickly revert back into their "at home" feeling. One study reveals that if they do not form six friendships within the first four to six months, most will leave the church. Those who become integrated into a small group are five times more likely to stay than those who do not find close relationships.

Watchman Nee writes, "The cross must do its work, reminding us that in Christ we have died to the old life of independence which we inherited from Adam, and that in the resurrection we have become not just an individual believer but a member of his Body. There is a vast difference between the two... The life of Christ in me will gravitate to the life of Christ in others. I can no longer take an individual line. Jealousy, competition will go. Private work will go. My interests, ambitions, preferences all will go. It will no long matter which of us does the work. All that will matter will be that the Body grows." [92]

The Church Should Be a Safe Place

The church is far from perfect. It's made up of messy sinners who hopefully love Jesus and love each other, a place where we bring our faults and sins, joys and hopes, guilt and shame, defeats and victories. We share our pain and celebrate our victories. If we are not vulnerable and open, our new friends will not feel safe. They think, "Everyone here has it all together. I'll never fit." We rejoice with those who rejoice and weep with those who weep. (Rom. 12:15). Paul writes in I Corinthians 9:22, "To the weak I become weak, to win the weak. I have become all things to all people so that by all possible means I might save some."

To have a welcoming community, we need to accept people like Jesus did. "You can't clean the fish before they get in the boat." Jesus accepted people before they believed and behaved: Levi and Zacchaeus the tax collectors, Simon the Zealot, the woman at the well, the woman caught in adultery, the twelve disciples and the demoniac, to name a few.

I try to warn every new person that our church is not perfect. We are human. Words and actions at times may be hurtful. Does that mean you should write church off as a lost cause? No! Jesus regularly went to the synagogue on the Sabbath. Synagogues were often corrupt, legalistic, and exclusive. Women were either not included or were considered second-class citizens. No church is perfect, but it is the best we have. Remember Christ loved the church and gave himself for her.

Transcendence

From the beginning of human history, humankind has worshiped something or someone. God has set eternity in the human heart. (Eccl. 3:11). Everyone needs something to live for beyond themselves. There are no atheists in foxholes. As Augustine said, "Our hearts are restless until they find rest in God." There is a God-sized hole in every heart. Transcendence gives us significance.

We are made in God's image and likeness, even the atheist who vehemently denies God. When Jesus entered the world, he brought true light to everyone. (Jn. 1:9). Out of the fullness of Christ everyone receives grace. (Jh. 1:16). We are all born with a conscience. People in every culture know intuitively it's wrong to push grandma in front of an oncoming train. Everyone needs faith in God.

In United States the number of atheists and agnostics has increased rapidly but worldwide the percentage of religious people is increasing. Science and technology, no matter how sophisticated, cannot satisfy our deep longing for "god." We must do all we can to bring them to faith in the only true God, our Lord and Savior Jesus Christ. (Jh. 17:3).

Belong, Believe and Behave

A welcoming and assimilating community accepts people like Jesus did. I grew up thinking a person had to first believe, second behave, and third, finally belong to the church community. We must change the order to first, belong, second, believe, and third, behave. Following this order results in a messy church. Is this order Biblical?

The unchurched can belong not in the sense of being a baptized member but in the sense of, "I feel love here; these are my people. I feel at home here."

Jesus accepted people before they believed and behaved. One of the most challenging verses in the Bible is Luke 15:1 (Msg.), "A lot of men and women of doubtful reputation were hanging around Jesus, listening intently." They liked to be with Jesus before they believed in him. Ask yourself, "Do prebelievers like to be around you?" Often pastors are kept so busy taking care of the sheep that they don't have time or take the time to build relationships in the world.

Was the "belong, believe, and behave" approach true in the New Testament Church? Listen to Paul's admonition to the Ephesian and Colossian Churches: Steal no longer; get rid of bitterness, rage, anger, brawling, slander, malice, dirty language, and evil desires; have not a hint of sexual immorality, impurity, lying, lust, greed, or drunkenness.

To the carnal church in Corinth he writes, "I am afraid I will find quarreling, jealousy, outbursts of anger, selfishness, backstabbing, gossip, conceit, and disorderly behavior. I grieve because many of you who sinned earlier have not repented of your impurity, sexual immorality and eagerness for lustful pleasure." (I Cor. 11:21; II Cor. 12:20-21).

When people become Christians they don't automatically become nice. The people of Corinth brought their bad habits with them into the church. Paul spent 18 months with them and then left. Later he received a report that things had fallen apart. He reminds them that Jesus is the answer. He takes them by the hand and goes over the old ground again, directing them in how to work God's saving love and grace into their lives and the life of the church.

Peter reminds them not to make it difficult for the Gentiles who are turning to God. (Ac. 15:19). It's interesting that the ones Jesus criticized the most were the Pharisees, those who thought they were pure by keeping their strict rules.

The problems we face with new people are a sign we are making progress in reaching the prebeliever. You don't want to leave people in their sinful habits, but when people really start engaging with Christ, the church gets messy like a hospital emergency room. Romans 15:7, "Accept one another, then, just as Christ accepted you, in order to bring praise to God."

Andy Stanley writes, "When you slow down long enough in your reading of Paul's epistles to consider the kinds of issues the early church wrestled with, you begin to realize just how messy the whole thing really was. When we choose to engage with culture at the level the Apostle Paul was forced to engage, it gets messy for us as well. It's the messy middle ground that makes some of us uncomfortable... There is something in us that would like a definitive answer on every nuance of every issue... I would argue that when we attempt to eliminate all the gray, all the messy middle ground, we end up with a poor caricature of what Christ originally intended when he announced his ekkleia. Actually we end up with multiple caricatures. And then we argue with each other over whose caricature is the true church."[93]

Holy and Pure Church

How can we reconcile the carnal characteristics found in all churches with the fact that Jesus is going to present a perfect and pure church to his Heavenly Father? Just as Jesus presents us as holy and pure before our Heavenly Father, even though we are sinful in our old nature, he presents the church, the body of Christ, as holy. Holiness is mandatory for us to enter heaven. "Without holiness no one will see the Lord." (Heb. 12:14). "God chose us in Christ... to be holy and blameless in his sight." (Eph. 1:3).

Just as Jesus presents a perfect church to his Father, he also presents us to God without fault. (Jude 24-25). Paul explains how we obtain our right standing before God in I Corinthians 1:31, "It is because of God that you are in Christ Jesus, who has become for us wisdom from God, i.e. our righteousness, holiness and redemption."

Concerning the church, Paul writes in Ephesians 5:26-27: "Jesus gave his life for the church to make her holy and clean. He washed her by the cleansing of water with the word. He did this to present her to himself as a glorious church without a spot or wrinkle or any other blemish. Instead she will be holy and without fault."

What Do We Do To Encourage People To Belong?

When new people come, what are we doing to encourage them to belong? We need to search our hearts to remove prejudices that hinder our spirits in welcoming and assimilating first-timers. We must ask ourselves as Rick Warren writes in, The Purpose Driven Church," (1) Do I really want to know these people, am I willing to spend time with them and love them? (2) Do I want them in my church? (3) Am I willing for my church to become their church? If so, how do they connect with the church? Do we have a process in place to follow-up on first-timers so they feel they are wanted?

What Are First-Timers Looking For?

They are asking themselves
- Is this church making a difference in our community; are lives being transformed by Christ?
- Do I fit here? Does anyone want to know me?
- Am I needed?
- What is required if I join?

How Do We Welcome First-Timers?

Do not refer to first-timers as strangers, visitors, or even new people. Call them "new friends" or "first-timers" implying they will return.

Most first-timers want to be anonymous. Do not publicly ask them to introduce themselves or have others introduce them. However, do your utmost to obtain each person's name, address, phone number, and email address. In small congregations you can do this informally either before or following the service.

In congregations of over 150 or 200, the worship leader extends a welcome to all those present, especially new friends or first-timers. He or she encourages everyone to remain for refreshments following the service. "For those who are new we especially welcome you to meet our friendly congregation around the refreshments, also we would like to send you a thank you note for coming. The ushers are coming down the aisle with a gift for you. Please hold up your hand so you can receive the gift. You will help us if you fill in your name and address on the card provided with the gift, and drop it in the offering plate or give it to an usher following the service." I've found it helpful to make the gift, perhaps a booklet, large enough so they can't hide it. Otherwise in larger congregations you may not remember they are first-timers until you see their gift. Welcome them.

The worship leader might also say, "Anyone who is interested in learning who we are, what we believe, and how we operate, please come to Room A down the hall to meet a few of our leaders who will answer questions and briefly introduce you to Entry Point 101. See your program for more details."

Provide Classes for Community People

When first-timers come, have a variety of options to peak their interest. List these opportunities in your program with the invitation to see anyone on the leadership team or an usher for more information. Examples are Youth Groups for Junior Highs and High Schoolers, and small groups meeting in various homes throughout the community, stating the primary focus of each group. Service projects such as helping a widow repair her porch or building a ramp for wheelchair access are less threatening ways to encourage them to participate. Other possibilities are cleaning up after a fire or fixing up a property near the church or any public building that needs some tender loving care. These hopefully communicate that your church cares not only about themselves but about their community. Inviting other congregations to work with you also communicates openness and acceptance. With some projects it is good not only to work with other churches but with community organizations.

New persons will seldom come for a series of studies. It's more helpful to offer seminars for one or two sessions. Examples might be flower arranging, ladies night out, photography, scrap booking, a trip to a ball game or Saturday brunch. On the other hand, if you have built a good relationship with the person you brought to church, he or she might be willing to participate in a series of classes: Bible overview, parenting, marriage enrichment, financial management, anger management, English as a Second Language, Elementary Spanish, exercise groups or church league sports.

Follow-up Summary

- Do your best to obtain your new friend's names, address, phone number, and email address
- Send a letter thanking them for coming
- Call or visit them later that week and thank them again for coming. If at all possible, have a short prayer remembering each of the children by name. Many parents have never experienced someone praying for their children. I have found this can soften their hearts and help draw them to the Christian faith.
- If they don't return the next Sunday, send them a program.
- If they don't return the following two or three Sundays, call again to thank them for coming and say, "Perhaps you have found a church; if not, I want to encourage you to return."

Tension: Serve Us or Serve Others

There is constant tension between the concept of "serve others" or "serve us." Most churches lean toward meeting members' needs because members pay the bills. Until we are mature enough to create a safe place for prebelievers at the expense of our own comfort and preferences, we will not be effective in assimilating new people. We must connect with them and give them a reason to return.

Practical Ways To Express Love

- People are God's guests, not strangers; they are first-timers or our new friends.
- Smile. It's absolutely amazing how Christians appear to have been baptized in lemon juice. Introduce yourself and offer your hand. Take the initiative. Touch is important. "Your face mirrors your heart." (Prov. 27:19).
- Look people in the eye.
- Learn their names.
- Ask what keeps them busy during the week. That's safer than asking if they are employed.
- Don't let people walk past you without noticing them. At least say, "Hi," or "Good morning" and SMILE.
- Have a time during the service to greet others.
- Sincere compliments are always helpful.
- Ask questions, but stay away from "why" questions.
- Show first-timers around, take them with you. Show them where the classroom, nursery and restrooms are located.
- Never let a first-timer stand or sit alone.
- Invite first-timers to other functions. Point these out in your weekly program.
- Turn the conversation to spiritual things. That's way they came, so don't be shy.
- Food is always appropriate.
- After they continue to show interest follow up with a letter, phone call, gifts, visits, etc..

Questions

1. Do you agree that there are a million miles between being friendly and being a friend? What hindrances do you experience in moving from being friendly to being a friend?
2. There are seventeen "one another" admonitions in the New Testament. Which ones do you find hard to practice? How might this be corrected?
3. Do you find it natural to help new persons know they are significant or know they are truly wanted? Give some illustrations how this is taking place in the life of your church.
4. Are you comfortable with the "Belong, Believe and Behave" concept presented in this chapter?
5. Does your church do well with following up new persons? How might you improve? Is the approach presented here assertive? How can improve your welcoming of first timers?
6. There is a constant tension between the concept of "serve others" or "serve us." Most churches lean toward meeting members' needs because members pay the bills. Until we are mature enough to create a safe place for prebelievers at the expense of our own comfort and preferences, we will not be effective in assimilating new people. Discuss.
7. What programs or activities does your church offer so new persons are tempted to return? Will these activities lead to making disciples who adopt the Great Commission as their passion?

14

A Word to Pastors and Leaders

"Everything rises or falls on leadership." John Maxwell

Needed: Men and Women of Conviction, Courage and Faith

Each month 1,500 pastors will leave the ministry entirely due to burnout or contention within their churches. And half of the pastors who stay, say they'd leave the ministry if they could find another job. They're stuck, and everyone else in the church is stuck with them. They know changes are needed, but they can't seem to get people unstuck enough to want or reach for better."[94]

Most leaders know what they need to do to reach the lost people and make disciples. They've taken seminars and heard accounts of dying churches that have been revitalized. The challenge is, "Do I have the courage to do what I know I need to do?" Many rightly fear they will lose their jobs if they make a paradigm shift moving from an internal focus to an external focus, making the Great Commission the compelling passion of their lives and the lives of their churches.

We must make disciples. (Matt. 28:18-20). The Lord didn't command us to build buildings or multiply members but to make disciples who walk with Jesus and become disciple makers. Leaders energized and empowered by the Holy Spirit are the catalysts to make this happen.

We Must Change Our Understanding of Church

We must change our understanding of church. Church structures may vary from small groups of persons meeting in homes to congregations with hundreds or thousands meeting in stadiums, whose people meet in small groups throughout the surrounding towns and cities. Some pastors are finding more fulfillment by leaving traditional church structures to begin Bible studies in homes or coffee shops, where it's easier for people to be transparent with one another.

Approximately fifty percent of pastors in the U.S. are bi-vocational. Half of the persons who attend church are in small congregations of seventy or less with the others in larger congregations or mega churches who have resources to support fulltime staff. In both the east and west coast the growth of mega churches has plateaued. As more pastors are "forced" to be bi-vocational we must identify and empower other gifted persons who can build up the body of Christ. This may well be God's plan for the future of his church in the U.S.

Convictions

Leaders must bring the following four convictions to the table. Questioning these convictions will undercut our motivation and passion for the Great Commission to be the compelling motivation of our lives.
- The Bible is the Word of God. (II Tim. 3:16-17).
- Jesus Christ is the Savior of the world and the only way to God. (Jn. 14:6-7).
- People must be saved to enter heaven. (Jn. 3:7).
- People without Christ are lost and headed for hell. (Jn. 3:36).

Values or Convictions

There is a huge difference between values and convictions. Gene Wood and Daniel Harkavy set forth the differences in their book, *Leading Turnaround Teams*.[95]

VALUES	CONVICTIONS
Will commit to ...	Will sacrifice for ...
Will contemplate the cost of ...	No cost is too great ...
Are negotiable ...	Non-negotiable ...
Ask others to subscribe ...	Expect/demand others to follow ...
Decided by the group ...	Decided by the individual ...
For a season ...	For a lifetime ...
Can be changed ...	Cannot be changed ...
External compliance acceptable ...	Internal ownership essential ...

"Christian leaders must express clearly what they believe, not as their own private speculations, but as authentic experience based on the Scriptures. Too many leaders do not want to alienate anyone, so they stay quiet on issues which cry out for leadership."[96] Without convictions and passion, leaders will burn out. This doesn't mean they should speak arrogantly. Jesus had convictions and yet he worked patiently with the "slow-learning" disciples. Leaders need to hold their convictions humbly, realizing they may not have all the light on any given situation.

I worked with several pastors who knew they needed to make changes but were not willing to risk moving forward. Some knew they needed to leave their rural setting and move into the nearby growing town, but the risk of seriously discussing this with the congregation was too great. I feel sure they will come to the end of their lives regretting their lack of faith by not being assertive in making the Great Commission the compelling passion in the live of their churches.

Vision

Many church problems arise because of our lack of vision. Our vision is too small to demand all our energies, so we manufacture petty problems to keep us busy.

Ask the pastors, elders, or church leaders in the vast majority of our churches, "What is God's vision for your church?" and there is silence. The status quo feels secure and comfortable. Henri Nouwen said, "Vision and mission are so central to the life of God's people that without vision we perish and without mission we lose our way." The older a church is, the more difficult it is to keep the vision.

If you can see how every aspect of your vision will be fulfilled, it is too small. If it does not require faith, it will not produce disciples. Don't be afraid to try new things. Call them an experiment and if they are unproductive, you haven't failed.

Vision Is Driven by the Great Commission

"Many leaders have never considered how their leadership is connected to the Great Commission. But God has given leaders a unique and strategic role in this task. Jesus gave this task first to His leadership team. He instructs his followers to go and make disciples of all nations. This happens when leaders see the goal, act on it, and share it with followers in a way that moves them to involvement as well. Without effective leadership, the Great Commission will not be accomplished. Every leadership position, including yours, is given by God to accomplish some part of fulfilling the Great Commission." [97]

A clear vision helps us say "no" to many legitimate ministries. We can't do everything. For example, a small church cannot begin a world-wide television ministry or a school, or offer a wide variety of classes simultaneously. It's helpful especially for smaller congregation to focus on one main mission project. This gives the congregation a special identity and recognition by everyone in their community. Examples might be: childcare, senior care, food pantry, clothing distribution, free meals certain days of the week, fixing up rundown houses, etc.

The focus of vision should be primarily outside the internal program of the church into the community and world. Some additional examples of a vision for smaller churches: to reach three families with children in the next year, to plant a new church every five years, to send a family into a foreign mission field in the next 24 months, or to have a least one member on the township school board.

Internal visions are easier to fulfill. Be very careful that your internal vision does not over shadow and weaken your external vision. Examples may be to train 50 percent of your people to share their faith in the next eight months, to have everyone read or listen to the New Testament in the next calendar year, to have all elementary children know the books of the Bible and at least ten key verses in this church calendar year, or to see that every youth in grades six to twelve has a mentor.

The task of discovering God's vision for your church may well be the most difficult job of the pastor and leadership team. The vision mutates and is shared with the leaders and the congregation. They give their godly wisdom and it becomes a team vision. Unless this happens, the church will not move forward.

Vision does at least four things: (1) vision increases energy and moves people into action, they can see where they are going and why they are giving their time and energy to this ministry; (2) vision increases ownership; (3) vision provides focus; and (4) vision assists evaluation. Unless there is honest evaluation the vision will not succeed.

Don't Neglect Community Involvement

Since the church has lost the respect of many in our culture the most effective way we can work at correcting this weakness is by getting involved in school activities and in community projects: food banks, sport leagues, clean-up days, help raise funds for the local hospital or the fire department, etc. People want to see the church making an impact for good in their community.

The Necessity of Faith

Every leader must have faith and vision. Moses sent the twelve spies, but only two, Joshua and Caleb, had vision. We remember them, but we don't remember the names of the ten. The ten men came up with many "reasons" they should not attempt to take the Promised Land. God punished the people for 40 years because of their lack of vision. (Num. 13-14).

"One of the sad things I have witnessed today is that people are afraid to step out in faith, lest they lose favor with their friends. So sadly, they dump down their vision. When a vision is merely palatable to a crowd, it requires no act of God... Set goals so big that unless God helps you, you will be a miserable failure."[98]

We all have to deal with feelings of failure. Fear of making changes is real. Some pastors will lose their jobs because the congregations will tenaciously resist the changes that are necessary to obey the Great Commission. Jesus said we can't put new wine in old wine skins. (Luke 5:37). That means there are times when leaders must be strong men and women with a willingness to leave the traditional church structure and begin with a group where the compelling passion is the Great Commission. It cost Jesus his life. As we earnestly pray for wisdom, he will give us courage to follow in his steps.

Out of the Study into the Streets

The focus of Jesus' ministry was training the twelve, but this training took place primarily in the world, not in the synagogue. We take Jesus' words more seriously than his actions. It's too easy for pastors to stay in their safe studies and tell the sheep they need to bring in new sheep and disciple them. Jesus, our Chief Shepherd, encountered people in the marketplace. We must do likewise. Sheep follow the leading of the shepherd.

My heart breaks when I see pastors absorbed in doing church work instead of the work of the church. Some spend endless hours making sure the weekly program is perfect, while the neighbors surrounding the church building don't know what the church is about. Pastors like Jesus' disciples are too often blind to the harvest around them. (Jn. 4:35-36). Pastors must have a bias for action in their community – action that grows out of passion to fulfill the Great Commission.

Most Christian leaders have very few prebeliever friends. This calls for a paradigm shift. This is a major challenge for most pastors, since their time is demanded by their church families. Many sit in their studies and counsel church people or wait for people to come to them. Unless the pastor or congregation is actively witnessing, the unchurched folks are not coming to the pastor's study today. Unless pastors have a strong conviction to reach the lost for Christ, they will not have the strength to go against the will of their members who demand their time. They will have a very difficult task to train their lay leaders and members to do the work of ministry either in the four walls or in the world. The members see this as the pastor's responsibility.

Pastors Must Lead the Way

When we hide ourselves in our church offices/studies, we find ourselves doing church work. The fatigue we feel is too often from doing church work. Church work will drain you. (Incidentally, do not call the church study your office. While there are some things we can learn from the business world, don't make office work your primary work. Your study is just that, a place to study God's word and a place of prayer to prepare the saints for their ministry.) (Ac. 6:4, Eph. 4:12).

If your church isn't growing, the most likely reason is that you're doing too much of the "urgent" stuff and not focusing on what is really important. Leaders, don't allow yourselves to become so busy taking care of the sick sheep that you do not have time to form relationships with the unchurched. As one church consultant suggested, "Make a list of what is important, the things that are in line with the Great Commission, and vow to do those things. Then make a list of things that are urgent but not as important and delegate those responsibilities to your lay leaders."

As we obey the Great Commission, people will come to faith. Seeing new families come into a relationship with Jesus, being baptized and discipled, encourages everyone. Some members, who have never invited anyone to Christ, will catch your passion and begin to courageously invite people to church.

The Need Is Great

There is no county in the continental United States where more than 15 percent of the population is in church on a Sunday morning. Passionate leaders remind themselves and their people that two out of seven people in our world, that's more than two billion people, have never heard the message of Jesus in a way that they can make a meaningful and valid response. Faithful leaders understand that Jesus' Great Commission compels them to build relationships with the unchurched, so they can hear the Good News and be discipled.

God's Blessing

I had the privilege of leading a discouraged group of 45 adults and children in an older, dying congregation to an attendance that frequently reached 400. We took the Great Commission seriously. People came; they shared their testimonies of new life in Jesus. The older, discouraged Christians caught the fire of the Holy Spirit and found the courage to invite their friends. To their surprise, they came.
There is nothing more exciting than experiencing a church where lives are being transformed. Life begets life. Life transformation is attractive and invigorating. People were being transferred from the kingdom of darkness to the Kingdom of Light; unbelievers became disciples. At one point, we had baptisms eight months in succession; nearly all were adults. More than once, people came and greeted me with the words, "What is it about this place? We felt it as we walked in from the parking lot." We were experiencing the inexpressible and glorious joy Peter talks about in I Peter 1:9. It was contagious.

In another church, I recorded my visits for the church leaders. I estimated that one-third of over 800 visits made that year were with the unchurched. In another urban setting, I may have slightly exaggerated when I commented, "I had more unsaved friends than I did church attenders." That was certainly true of Jesus. (Lk. 15:1).

Presently I am relating to a former professional boxer and a former bull rider. What a joy to see these lives being slowly transformed into the image of Christ.

Jesus Said, "Feed My Sheep"

Just before Jesus ascended to heaven, he told Peter, "Feed my sheep." If we feed the congregation year after year, and they are not making disciples who make disciples, are we truly feeding the congregation? If it takes 84 Christians in America to bring one person to Jesus in a year's time, the "feed" is not being translated into their daily living.

> The preaching of the gospel has become so watered down that the non-elect can't even reject it. If you don't have people walking away from your ministry saying, "This is a hard word, who can accept it?" then you don't have a ministry like Jesus had.

> I just hate this notion that we can be so clever and sophisticated that we can remove the offense from the gospel. It is foolishness to those who are perishing; it is the power of God to those who are being saved. It is the aroma of death to those who are perishing; it is the aroma of life to those who are being saved.

> Listen, preacher: if you don't want to be the aroma of death to those who are perishing, you can never be the aroma of life to those who are being saved. That's why preaching is hard work. [99]

Shepherds Don't Have Sheep?

Some say, "Shepherds don't have sheep, sheep have sheep." This analogy is not applicable. Unless the Shepherd is modeling reaching out to the unchurched, the members will not be sharing the Good News. Leaders are to equip the believers. Consequently, they will need to say "no" to many internal church activities to give the Great Commission the priority that Jesus intended. Paul instructed Timothy to preach the word, but he also instructed him to do the work of an evangelist. (II Tim. 4:1-5).

Fear Is Frequent

Many leaders are fearful of leaving their studies. They are extremely hesitant to invite people they don't know to church. Some admit they have no unsaved friends. On the other hand, some pastors have good rapport with the unchurched, but they do not have the boldness or passion of Peter and John to share the Good News. Too often, their conversations involve ball scores, the stock market, new cars or politics and the world situation, but they never get around to introducing the truth of Jesus or even to invite the unchurched to worship with them.

The most exciting place in a hospital is the maternity ward. The same is true in our churches. Apparently heaven has the same opinion, since all heaven rejoices when the lost sheep and the prodigal son return home. (Lk. 15). The party is not limited to heaven; it spills over into our congregations as well.

Some Helpful Strategies

Bill Tenny-Brittian writes, "You can do one of two things. You can focus on trying to fix what's broken so that you end up with a "healthy" church. On the other hand, the alternative is to focus on those things that grow churches and deal with the broken things as they come up and get in the way. Those four things that grow a church are:

A Robust Inviting Strategy

Growing churches have a robust inviting strategy. They not only see a steady stream of first-time visitors but a stream of baptisms as well.

An Effective Connecting Strategy

In churches without an effective connecting strategy, only fifteen percent of their first-time visitors return and half of those will drop within a year. Churches with an effective connecting strategy boost their return and retention rate to well over fifty percent.

A Comprehensive Discipleship Strategy

Growing churches have a comprehensive discipleship strategy that gets beyond the intellect and taps into the emotions, but even more so, helps their members change their behavior.

A Compelling Sending Strategy

Growing churches have a strategy for going and making such a difference in the community that it energizes the average person in the pew and compels them to faithful missional action.[100]

Leaders' Most Formidable Challenge

As a pastor, I had to learn that sending workers is integral to making disciples. We invested time and energy and watched our workers develop into leaders, who then moved on for greater ministry.

We must release, bless, pray and provide some support for those we send into the mission field, whether it is planting a church five miles away or serving on the other side of the world. We don't send them out alone. They need emotional, physical, financial, and above all our spiritual support.

One of my greatest joys as a pastor was discipling and equipping men and women to serve in other locations. I wish I would have given more of my time to this important ministry.

Ron Byler from Global Disciples writes,

> Pastors may need to release their best elder to a new location. Business owners may be called to release an excellent manager from their company to serve in another place, where the light of Jesus is needed. It is not easy for any leader who has invested time and energy in the life of someone to see them move on. It requires the heart of a servant who is intent not on building his own kingdom, but that of the Father.
>
> The work of the Great Commission requires resources. This may include training harvest workers to be self-supporting or it may include providing financial support for their work. Paul demonstrates both models of support in his church planting efforts. Leaders who focus all their energy on their own organization will not be willing to give resources to an 'outside' cause. But servant leaders... freely and cheerfully give to support local initiatives in which God's kingdom is extended and also eagerly give to workers who are reaching the 2 billion who have not yet heard. They do not see this giving as a drain on their own resources; instead they eagerly ask God to give them ideas and ways to increase their own ability to give. Pastors look for ways that they can increase the percentage of their budget to areas directly related to the Great Commission. Business leaders give generously as God blesses their work and sometimes begin a business with the sole intent of using the profit for the Great

Commission. Professionals are careful to invest portions of their income into Great Commission work... [101]

We must be a sending church. Jesus was sent. We are sent. (Jn. 17-18, 20:21). The word "sent" or "sent" appears nearly sixty times in the book of John. Churches commission those going into long-term missions. We need to realize we are commissioned and sent with all authority and power in our home communities as well. Everyone is to be a missionary in his or her local community. The attraction model is not longer effective. We must be a sending church!

Leaders Must Deal with Conflict

Change and conflict seem to go hand-in-hand. Those that want the church to stay with the status quo are often older persons who pay the bills. If you stay with the status quo, your church will most likely decline. You will lose some people who want changes. If you make changes, you will lose some who don't want the changes. Attempting to work a compromise often means that neither side is satisfied. You will lose some on both camps. You are being tested.

People change, culture changes, the Gospel doesn't change; but how we communicate the Gospel must be relevant to the culture.

Perhaps those who drop out are doing you a favor. If they are not happy, they will drag down the vision, create tension, and stymie the Holy Spirit. When people walked away from Jesus, he did not go after them. As difficult as it is, bless those who leave. Pray and release them to find a place where they are more comfortable.

Passion Is the Key

As I said at the beginning, the basic ingredient of a disciple is Godly passion to fulfill the Great Commandment and the Great Commission. Listen to Paul's passion one more time: "I have great sorrow and unceasing anguish in my heart. For I could wish that I myself were cursed and cut off from Christ for the sake of my people." (Ro. 9:2-3). The Holy Spirit will give us passion for the lost. We must rise to a new level of faith and be willing to go out on the limb where it is risky, but that's the only place to bear fruit. Be men and women of the word, (Chapter 5), men and women filled with the Holy Spirit, (Chapter 6), and men and women of prayer, (Chapter 7), who live a God-given vision.

Obtaining Godly Passion

Pray with David, "Search me, God, and know my heart; test me and know my anxious thoughts. See if there is any offensive way in me and lead me in the way everlasting." (Ps. 139:23-24). Confess any known sin. Bring every thought in line with God's Holy Spirit. (I Cor. 2:16b and II Cor. 10:4-5). Tell God every moment is his to use. Your will is his will. I pray each day that I will do only what pleases the Father; not my will but his. God will light a fire in your bones. He will empower you beyond what you ask or imagine according to his power that is at work in you. (Eph. 3:20).

Where Do We Go?

How do you find where God wants you to go? Pray! Where is God leading you? What are your passions? All members have relatives, acquaintances, neighbors and work peers who are unchurched, yet many never share God's love with them. Some of these people are living in a crisis mode. While some members may not have the courage to share the Good News, they may be willing to introduce you as their pastor to relate to these hurting persons. This is far from the New Testament ideal, but it can be a starting point to reach many new families and disciple them. Some who were too inhibited to share Jesus will catch the vision and find the courage to share Jesus.

Coffee shops, malls, parks, sporting events, and community clubs are all places where you can meet persons to build relationships. As the Holy Spirit leads, share the Good News of Jesus. Many persons are on the margins of your community. Some of them will respond to God's love if you meet a need in their lives and show persistent love.

Questions:

1. Have you made the Great Commission the compelling passion of your life? If not, what is holding you back?
2. Do you agree, that if we are people of Godly zeal and passion, God will give direction in our ministry so we can relate to others as Jesus did? (Ro. 12:11).
3. Have you succumbed to the culture which says that it is not politically correct to share your faith in Jesus Christ? Do you agree this has resulted in a lukewarm Christianity?
4. Bill Tenny-Brittian writes, "You can focus on trying to fix what's broken so that you end up with a "healthy" church. Or you can focus on those things that grow churches and deal with the broken things as they come up and get in the way." Discuss.
5. Tenny-Brittian lists these four things that grow a church: (1) a robust inviting strategy, (2) an effective connecting strategy, (3) a comprehensive discipleship strategy, and (4) a compelling sending strategy. Which one(s) does God want you to focus on?
6. What is God asking you to do to step out in faith to fulfill the Great Commission? Can you name a work peer or a friend with whom you need to share the Good News? Will you ask others to pray for you as you witness to them?
7. Where is the Holy Spirit nudging you to go to share your faith? Is going to a coffee shop, mall, park, sporting event, family reunion or community club a place where you can meet people, build relationships and eventually share Jesus?
8. Since the most effective way to impact our communities is to get involved in community life, how might you or your church become more involved in your community?

Concluding Challenge

Few Christians deeply desire to share the Good News. When Christians merely attend church and serve their own needs, they are like the Dead Sea, taking in but not giving out. Since God is a loving God, they assume, "If I just live a good life and help my friends, I'll be fine."

Do you think the good works of Muslims, Buddhists, Hindus, atheists and agnostics earn them an entrance into heaven? It's impossible to earn salvation by living a good life and doing good works. Unless we repent we will perish. (Lk. 13:1-5). No one can come to the Father except through Jesus. (Jn. 14:6-7, Acts 4:12, I Tim. 2:5 and Jude 25).

Jesus' motivation is to reach the dying world with the transforming Good News of the Gospel. As the Father sent him, he sends us. The Great Commission is for all Christians. His commission must be the passion that motivates and compels our lives. It begins at home, in our Jerusalem, and extends to the ends of the earth.

There are more than one billion people who are living without adequate food and water. Will we tell them the Good News by providing nourishing, nutritious food and safe drinking water, by providing housing for the homeless and providing basic medical help? Most Christians would say, "Yes." That is the delusion Satan has propagated in the church today. The secular culture, along with the vast majority of Christians, loves this approach. Christians will support it by quoting Jesus' words in Matthew 25:31-46: feed the hungry, give water to the thirsty, provide shelter for the homeless, clothes for those who need clothes, and visit those who are sick or in prison. These good acts must come from a heart of love for Jesus that overflows in *both* deeds and words. We must practice what we preach, but we must also preach what we practice to fulfill the Great Commission.

We cannot make disciples as Jesus commissions us, unless we have a Christ-centered passion for the lost. This passion drives our desire to know Jesus intimately, to diligently study his Word, to pray fervently, and to follow the leading of the Holy Spirit; then out of us will flow rivers of living water to a thirsty world.

It's my prayer that this book will move us out from behind our four walls to take the Good News of Jesus with a heart of love and a life of service to our relatives, neighbors, communities and to the ends the earth. "This gospel of the Kingdom will be preached in the whole world as a testimony to all nations, and then the end will come." (Matt. 24:14).

God has done his part. The question before us: "Will we do our part?"

* * * * * * * *

As I was finishing this book I dreamt I was in a church service. As the service ended I found myself standing alone. I remembered seeing a few people that I met before but they left without noticing me. I felt alone. Then I found myself talking with the elders of the church. During our conversation I asked how many baptisms they had this past year. They appeared discourage and didn't answer. It was dusk now. I needed a "home." They gave me a ride in the back seat of their car and dropped me off along the road. It was chilly, cloudy and getting dark. I so wished they would have offered to take me where I could find "home." The first house I saw appeared to be empty, the shades were pulled and the windows were dark. As I walked on in the darkness I found myself with another person. We walked together until they entered their home. I walked on feeling lost and abandoned. Another person appeared. I walked with them until they entered what appeared to be a well kept house and property. I was alone again! The next house was dark but a man appeared. I told him I was lost and needed a place to stay. We stood there in the cold darkness as I longed for him to invite me "home." Who will you invite "home" today?

Appendix

Assessment Exercise

This tool can facilitate discussion concerning a congregation's perspective and focus. Each item below has two statements about attitudes in the congregation. Circle the number you feel best describes your congregation's perspective. A "one" indicates total agreement with the statement on the left, while "five" indicates total agreement with the statement on the right.

Unhealthy   **Healthy**

1. Cares mostly for those in the church   Cares for insiders and outsiders
   1   2   3   4   5

2. Visitors are strangers   Visitors are guests of God
   1   2   3   4   5

3. Keeps things the same   Flexible
   1   2   3   4   5

4. Insiders versus outsiders   We are for the outsider
   1   2   3   4   5

5. Church facility is for us   Facilities for others too
   1   2   3   4   5

6. Prayer mostly for ourselves   Prayer for ourselves and unchurched
   1   2   3   4   5

7. Occasional mission projects   Everyone is a missionary
   1   2   3   4   5

8. Emphasize getting it right   Try, evaluate, learn from mistakes
   1   2   3   4   5

9. Long-standing committees   Flexible teams

      1   2   3   4   5

10. Budget dictates ministry   Ministry first, funds last

      1   2   3   4   5

11. Identified by our heritage   Identified by beliefs, values and ministry

      1   2   3   4   5

12. One big, happy family   Christ's community reaching the
unchurched and discipling them

      1   2   3   4   5

13. Being a member   Being a disciple

      1   2   3   4   5

14. Goal: more members   Goal: making disciples

      1   2   3   4   5

15. Saving for a rainy day   Now is the time

      1   2   3   4   5

16. Funds: we have little   Funds: God has given much

      1   2   3   4   5

17. We give to missions   Missions: everything we are and do

      1   2   3   4   5

18. Missions: somewhere   Missions: here and the world

      1   2   3   4   5

19. Missions: one of many programs   Missions: the central organizing purpose

      1   2   3   4   5

20. More than half of money, energy leadership, attention, and prayers are spent on members.   More than half for those outside
the church

      1   2   3   4   5

Working through one of the following exercises will also help determine if your congregation is willing to become more missional.

(1) In *Breakout Churches*, Thom Rainer includes a Church Readiness Inventory to help congregations determine if they are ready to become missional. (241-244).

(2) A twenty-question readiness tool in *Advanced Strategic Planning* by Aubrey Malphurs will also help you discern if your church is ready to move ahead with revitalization. (270-278).

End Notes

Introduction

[1] Steve Sjorgren and Dave Ping, *Out Flow: Outward-focused Living in a Self-focused World* (Loveland, CO: Group Publishing, 2006), 158.

[2] Jim Denison, "A Surprising Strategy for Reaching Our Culture" (DenisonForum.com, 2/3/2015).

[3] Bruce Roberts Dreisbach, *The Jesus Plan* (Colorado Springs, CO: Waterbrook, 2002), 28.

[4] Ibid.

[5] Jim Denison, "How To Change Your Culture" (DenisonForum.com, 11/2/2014).

[6] Dreisbach, *The Jesus Plan*, 59.

[7] Neil Cole, *Organic Church* (San Francisco, CA: Jossey-Bass, 2005), 31.

[8] Bill Tenny-Brittian and Bill Easum, "How Congregations Stymie Church Growth" (21st Century Strategies email, 8/24/2012).

[9] Paul Billheimer, *Destined for the Throne* (Fort Washington, PA: Christian Literature Crusade, 1976), 89.

[10] globalmediaoutreach.com

[11] thetravelingteam.org

Chapter 1

[12] Andy Stanley, *Deep and Wide* (Grand Rapids, MI: Zondervan, 2012), 59.

[13] Cole, Organic Church, 53.

[14] Craig Groeschel, *The Christian Atheist* (Grand Rapids, MI: Zondervan, 2010), 222.

[15] Oswald Chambers, *My Utmost for His Highest* (Grand Rapids, MI: Discovery House Publishers, 1992), January 31 reading.

[16] Floyd McClung, *You See Bones, I See an Army* (Colorado Springs, CO: YWAM & DavidCook Publishers, 2007), 129.

[17] This section was adapted from John M. Drescher's article "When was the Switch Made?" (Unpublished, 2009).

[18] Brandon Hatmaker, *Barefoot Church* (Grand Rapids, MI: Zondervan, 2011), 150.

[19] K. P. Yohannan, *Revolution in World Missions* (Carrollton, TX: gfa books, a division of Gospel for Asia, 1986; 38th printing 2011), 168-170.

Chapter 4

[20] David Platt. *Radical*. 70-71.
[21] Mike Bickle, "What's Wrong with Grace?" (Charisma Magazine, April 2013), 28.

[22] David Platt, *Radical* (Colorado Springs, CO: Multnomah Books, 2010), 29.
[23] NIV/The Message Parallel Study Bible, Introduction to Zephaniah (Grand Rapids, MI: Zondervan, 2008), 1843.
[24] Yohannan, *Revolution in World Missions*, 94-95.
[25] Ted Haggard, *Primary Purpose* (Orlando, FL: Creation House, 1995), 174.
[26] Denison, "How to Change Your Culture."
[27] Mark Driscoll, "Who Is Jesus?" (Sermon Central.com, 3/13/2013).
[28] Bill Bright, *The Journey Home* (Nashville, TN: Thomas Nelson Publishers, 2003), 167.
[29] Denison, "A Surprising Strategy for Reaching Our Culture."

Chapter 5

[30] William Barclay, *The Acts of the Apostles* (Edinburgh, Saint Andrews Press, 1955), 25.
[31] Brad Lomerick, "The Catalyst Leader: 8 Essentials for becoming a Change Maker" (Sermon Central.com, 4/19/2013), Chapter 3.
[32] Cole, *Organic Church*, 67.
[33] Platt, *Radical*, 27-28.
[34] Dennis McCallum, *Members of One Another* (New Paradigm Publishing, 2010), 158.
[35] Don Jacobs, *Into All the World*, quoted from the Interpreter's Bible, 258.

Chapter 6

[36] Cole, *Organic Church*, 50.
[37] Platt, *Radical*, 59-60.
[38] Brother Yun, *Living Water* (Grand Rapids, MI: Zondervan, 2008), 59.
[39] Jim Denison, "The Great Evangelical Recession" (DenisonForum.com, 1/5/2015).
[40] Angie Williams, *Jesus Wants Your Mind* (Kearney, NE: Morris Publishing, 2012), 16.
[41] Jacobs, *Into All the World* (Lancaster, PA: Global Disciples, 2014), 274.
[42] Charles Hodge, *Systematic Theology* (Oak Harbor, WA: Logus Research Systems, Inc, 1997), quoted in McCallum, Members of One Another, 14.
[43] Cole, *Organic Church*, 30-31.

Chapter 7

[44] Brad Brisco and Lance Ford, *Missional Essentials*. 54.
[45] Andrew Murray, *With Christ in the School of Prayer* (Grand Rapids, MI: Fleming H. Revell, 1953), 8.
[46] Ibid., 72-73.
[47] Billheimer, *Destined for the Throne,* 40.
[48] Murray, *With Christ in the School of Prayer*, 52.
[49] Jacobs, Into All the World, 184-185.
[50] Joel Comiskey, *Biblical Foundations for the Cell-Based Church* (Edmond, OK: CCS Publishing, 2012), Chapter 5.
[51] David Platt, *Radical Together*, (Colorado Springs, CO: Multnomah, 2011), 114.
[52] Heidi Baker, Compelled by Love (Lake Mary, FL: Charisma House, 2008), 69.

[53] Yun, *Living Water*, 132.

[54] Jon Byler, "Reflections for Servant Leaders" (Global Disciples Newsletter, Issue 95, 12/4/2012).

[55] Yohannan, *Revolution in World Mission*, 89-90.

[56] Murray, *With Christ in the School of Prayer*, 74.

[57] Peter Wagner, *Engaging the Enemy* (Ventura, CA: Regal Books, 1991), 79.

[58] Bill Bright, quoted in James Montgomery, I'm Gonna Let it Shine! (Colorado Springs, CO: Dawn Ministries, 2001), 147.

[59] David Platt, *Radical Together*, 43.

[60] Billheimer, *Destined for the Throne*, 50.

[61] Ibid., 51.

[62] Platt, *Radical Together*, 14-15.

[63] Murray, *With Christ in the School of Prayer,* 23.

[64] Billheimer, *Destined for the Throne*, 133.

[65] Cole, *Organic Church*, 51-52.

[66] Edwin Orr, *The Role of Prayer in Spiritual Awakening*, Oxford Association for Research in Revival. 8.

Chapter 8

[67] Platt, *Radical*, 111.

[68] Groeschel, *The Christian Atheist*, 198-200.

[69] Platt, *Radical*, 73.

[70] Ed Silvoso, *That None Should Perish* (Ventura, CA: Regal Books, 1994), 91-92.

[71] Ryan Pemberton, Called: My Journey to C. S. Lewis's House and Back Again (Abilene, TX: Leafwood Publishing, 2015), 58-59.

[72] Jim Denison, "Shout Your Abortion or Share Your Faith" (DenisonForum.com, 9/25/2015).

Chapter 9

[73] John Drescher, "When Was the Switch Made?"

[74] Pemberton, *Called: My Journey to C. S. Lewis's House*, 56.

[75] Ed Stetzer, "Preach the Gospel, and Since It's Necessary, Use Words" (SermonCentral.com, 10/8/2014).

[76] Yohannan, Revolution in World Missions, 109.

[77] Yun, *Living Water*, 170, 189.

[78] I am indebted to Dennis McCallum's book *Members of One Another* for many of the ideas presented in this image of the church. 61-66.

[79] Dennis McCallum, *Members of One Another,* 64.

[80] Brother Lawrence, *The Practice of the Presence of God* (New Kensington, PA: Whitaker House, 1982), 14-17.

Chapter 10

[81] John Piper, "Share the Good News" (SermonCentral.com, 10/18/2013).

Chapter 11

[82] Jim Denison, "Good News for Born-again Christians" (DenisonForum.com, 5/13/2015).
[83] Jacobs, *Into All the World*, 276.
[84] Rick Rusaw and Eric Swanson, *The Externally Focused Church* (Loveland, CO: Group Publishing, 2004), 82-83.

Chapter 12

[85] Brisco and Ford, *Missional Essentials*, 61.
[86] Bristle and Ford, *Missional Essentials,* 61-62. [87] Sims, George Mueller: Man of Faith. 16.

[88] Chambers, *My Utmost for His Highest*, Oct. 26 reading.
[89] Rusaw and Swanson, *The Externally Focused Church*, 51.
[90] Rusaw and Swanson, *The Externally Focused Church*, 7.
[91] Brandon O'Brien, "The Strategically Small Church" (SermonCentral.com, 3/18/15).

Chapter 13

[92] Dennis McCallum quotes Watchman Nee, *The Normal Christian Life*, (Hong Kong: Christian Literature Crusade, 1971), 218-219 in Members of One Another, 20-21.
[93] Stanley, *Deep & Wide*, 72-73.

Chapter 14

[94] Craig Cable, "Are More Pastors Becoming 'Done' with Church?" (DenisonForum.com, 2/9/15).
[95] Wood and Harkavy, *Leading Turnaround Teams*, 28.
[96] Jacobs, *Into All the World*, 222.
[97] Jon Byler, "Servant Leaders" (Global Disciples Newsletter, Issue 150, 3/4/2015).
[98] Bright, *The Journey Home*, 99-102.
[99] James McDonald, "Five Things To Do Today Instead of Preaching the Word" (SermonCentral.com, 5/28/2015).
[100] Bill-Tenny-Brittian, "Only Four Things Grow Churches" (HorizonsStewardship.com, 4/24/2014).
[101] Ron Byler, "Servant Leaders and the Great Commission" (Global Disciples email, 4/1/2015).

Bibliography

Baker, Heidi. *Compelled by Love*. Lake Mary, FL: Charisma House, 2008.

Barclay, William. *Gospel of Matthew Vol.1*. Edinburgh: Saint Andrews Press, 1958.

Barclay, William. *The Acts of the Apostles*. Edinburgh: Saint Andrews Press, 1955.

Barna, George. *Leaders on Leadership: Wisdom, Advice, and Encouragement on the Art of Leading God's People*. Ventura, CA: Regal Books, 1997.

Barrett, Lois Y., ed. *Treasure in Clay Jars: Patterns in Missional Faithfulness*. Grand Rapids, MI: Eerdmans, 2004.

Bickle, Mike. "What's Wrong with Grace?" Charisma Magazine, April 2013.

Billheimer, Paul E. *Destined for the Throne: A New Look at the Bride of Christ*. Fort Washington, PA: Christian Literature Crusade, 1976.

Bright, Bill. *The Journey Home*. Nashville, TN: Thomas Nelson Publishers, 2003.

Brisco, Brad, and Lance Ford, *Missional Essentials, The House Studio*, Kansas City, MO. 64141. 2012.

Byler, Jon. "Reflections from Servant Leaders." Global Disciples Newsletter, Issue 89, 9/29/2012.

————. "Reflections for Servant Leaders." Global Disciples Newsletter, Issue 95, 12/4/2012.

————. "Servant Leaders." Global Disciples Newsletter, Issue 150, 3/4/2015.

Byler, Ron. "Servant Leaders and the Great Commission. Global Disciples email. 4/1/2015.

Chambers, Oswald. *My Utmost for His Highest*. Grand Rapids, MI: Discovery House Publishers, 1992.

Chan, Francis. *Forgotten God*. Peabody, MA: David C. Cook, 2009.

Claiborne, Shane, *Irresistible Revolution*, Zondervan, 2006.

Clegg, Tom, and Warren Bird. *Lost in America: How You and Your Church Can Impact the World Next Door*. Loveland, CO: Group Publishing, 2001.

Cole, Neil. *Organic Church*. San Francisco, CA: Jossey-Bass, 2005.

Coleman, Robert. *The Master Plan of Evangelism*. Old Tappan, NJ: Spire Books, 1964.

Comiskey, Joel. *Biblical Foundations for the Cell-Based Church*. Edmond, OK: CCS Publishing, 2012.

Crossman, Meg. *Perspectives Exposure: Discovering God's Heart for All Nations and Our Part in His Plan*. Seattle, WA: YWAM Publishing, 2003.

Daniel, Orville E. *A Harmony of the Four Gospels*, New International Version. Grand Rapids, MI: Baker Book House, 1973.

Davis, Diana. *Fresh Ideas: 1,000 Ways to Grow a Thriving and Energetic Church*. Nashville, TN: B&H Publishing Group, 2007.

Davis, O. James. "32 Quotes on Effective Preaching." SermonCentral.com, December 2007.

Dawson, John. *Taking Our Cities for God: How to Break Spiritual Strongholds*. Lake Mary, FL: Creation House, 1971.

Denison, Jim. "A Surprising Strategy for Reaching Our Culture." DenisonForum.com, 2/3/2015.

———. "Good News for Born-again Christians." DenisonForum.com, 5/13/2015.

———. "How to Change Your Culture." DenisonForum.com, 11/2/2014.

———. Share Your Faith." DenisonForum.com, 9/25/2015.

———. "The Great Evangelical Recession." DenisonForum.com, 1/5/2015.

Dreisbach, Bruce Robert. *The Jesus Plan*. Colorado Springs, CO: Waterbrook, 2002.

Drescher, John M. "When Was the Switch Made?" Unpublished article, 2009.

Driscoll, Mark. "Who is Jesus?" SermonCentral.com, 3/13/2013.

Eareckson Tada, Joni. *Pearls of Great Price*. Grand Rapids, MI: Zondervan, 2006.

Eshleman, J. David. *Now Go Forward: Reaching Out to Grow Your Congregation*. Scottdale, PA: Herald Press, 2009.

Fletcher, Michael. *Overcoming Barriers to Growth: Proven Strategies for Taking Your Church to the Next Level*. Minneapolis, MN: Bethany House, 2006.

Global Media Outreach website (globalmediaoutreach.com).

Groeschel, Craig. *The Christian Atheist*. Grand Rapids, MI: Zondervan, 2010.

Hatmaker, Brandon. *Barefoot Church*. Grand Rapids, MI: Zondervan, 2011.

Haggard, Ted. *Primary Purpose: Making It Hard for People to Go to Hell from Your City*. Orlando, FL: Creation House, 1995.

Hattaway, Paul. *Back to Jerusalem: Called to Complete the Great Commission*. Waynesboro, GA: Gabriel Publishing, 2003.

Hybels, Bill. *Holy Discontent: Fueling the Fire That Ignites Personal Vision*. Grand Rapids, MI: Zondervan, 2007.

————. *Just Walk Across the Room*. Grand Rapids, MI: Zondervan, 2006.

Jacobs, Don. *Into All the World: A Commentary on Acts for Cross-Culture Workers*. Lancaster, PA: Global Disciples, 2014.

Johnson, Jeff. *How to Hug a Smelly Man*. Bloomington, IN: WestBow Press, 2012.

Kanagy, Conrad L. *Road Signs for the Journey: A Profile of Mennonite Church USA*. Scottdale, PA: Herald Press, 2007.

Kimball, Dan. *The Emerging Church: Vintage Christianity for New Generations*. Grand Rapids, MI: Zondervan, 2003.

————. *They Like Jesus but Not the Church: Insights from Emerging Generations*. Grand Rapids, MI: Zondervan, 2007.

Lawrence, Brother. *The Practice of the Presence of God*. New Kensington, PA: Whitaker House, 1982.

Lawson, Steve. "Is it Necessary to Preach Divine Wrath?" SermonCentral. com, 6/5/2015.

Lomerick, Brad. "The Catalyst Leader: 8 Essentials for Becoming a Church Maker." SermonCentral.com, 4/19/2013.

Malphurs, Aubrey. *Advanced Strategic Planning: A New Model for Church and Ministry Leaders*. Grand Rapids, MI: Baker Books, 2005.

McCallum, Dennis. *Members of One Another*. New Paradigm Publishing, 2010.

McClung, Floyd. *You See Bones, I See an Army*. Colorado Springs, CO: YWAM & David Cook Publishers, 2007.

McDonald, James. "Five Things to Do Today Instead of Preaching the Word."SermonCentral.com, 5/28/2015.

McIntosh, Gary L. *One Size Doesn't Fit All: Bringing Out the Best in Any Size Church*. Grand Rapids, MI: Fleming H. Revell, 1999.

McKaughan, Paul. "MissioNexus." Email (Info@MissioNexus.org), 8/20/2012.

Mittelberg, Mark, and Bill Hybels. *Becoming a Contagious Christian*. Grand Rapids, MI: Zondervan, 1995.

Montgomery, James. *I'm Gonna Let it Shine!* Colorado Springs, CO: Dawn Ministries, 2001.

Murray, Andrew. *With Christ in the School of Prayer*. Grand Rapids, MI: Fleming H. Revell, 1953.

Nee, Watchman. *The Normal Christian Life*. England: Christian Literature Crusade, 1957.

NIV/*The Message Parallel Study Bible*, Introduction to Zephaniah. Grand Rapids, MI: Zondervan, 2008.

O'Brien, Brandon. "The Strategically Small Church." SermonCentral.com, 3/18/2015.

Orr, Edwin, *The Role of Prayer in Spiritual Awakening*. Oxford Association for Research in Revival, 11451 Berwick St. Los Angeles, CA 90049.

Pemberton, Ryan. *Called: My Journey to C. S. Lewis's House and Back Again*. Abilene, TX: Leafwood Publishing, 2015.

Piper, John. "Share the Good News." SermonCentral.com, 10/18/2013.

Platt, David. *Radical*. Colorado Springs, CO: Multnomah Books, 2010.

———. *Radical Together*. Colorado Springs, CO: Multnomah Books, 2011.

Rainer, Thom S. *Breakout Churches: Discover How to Make the Leap*. Grand Rapids, MI: Zondervan, 2005.

Rainer, Thom and Sam Rainer III. *Essential Church: Reclaiming a Generation of Dropouts*. Nashville, TN: B&H Publishing Group, 2008.

Rusaw, Rick, and Eric Swanson. *The Externally Focused Church.* Loveland, CO: Group Publishing, 2004.

Schmidt, Wayne. *Ministry Momentum: How to Get It, Keep It, and Use It in Your Church.* Indianapolis, IN: Wesleyan Publishing House, 2004.

Scott, John. "The Living God is a Missionary God." Quoted in Perspectives Exposure, by Meg Crossman. Louisville, KY: YWAM, 2003.

Silvoso, Ed. *That None Should Perish: How to Reach Entire Cities for Christ through Prayer Evangelism.* Ventura, CA: Regal Books, 1994.

Sims, A. George Muller: *Man of Faith.* Wipf & Stock, Eugene, Oregon, 79401. 2005

Sjogren, Steve. *101 Ways to Reach Your Community.* Colorado Springs, CO: NavPress, 2001.

Sjogren, Steve, and Dave Ping. *Outflow: Outward-focused Living in a Self-focused World.* Loveland, CO: Group Publishing, 2006.

Stanley, Andy. *Deep and Wide.* Grand Rapids, MI: Zondervan, 2012.

Stearns, Richard, *The Hole in our Gospel,* Thomas Nelson, Nashville, 2010.

Stetzer, Ed, and David Putman. *Breaking the Missional Code: Your Church Can Become a Missionary in Your Community.* Nashville, TN: Broadman and Holman Publishers, 2006.

Stetzer, Ed. "Preach the Gospel, and Since It's Necessary, Use Words." SermonCentral.com, 10/8/2014.

Stevenson, Phil. *The Ripple Church.* Indianapolis, IN: Wesleyan Publishing House, 2004.

Sullivan, Bill M. *Ten Steps to Breaking the 200 Barrier.* Kansas City, MO: Beacon Hill Press, 1988.

Tenny-Brittian, Bill and Bill Easum. "How Congregations Stymie Church Growth." 21st Century Strategies email, 8/24/2012.

Tenny-Brittian, Bill. "Only Four Things Grow Churches." HorizonsSteward-ship.com, 4/24/2014

The Traveling Team Inc. website (thetravelingteam.org).

Trebilcock, Robin J. *The Small Church at Large: Thinking Local in a Global Context*. Nashville, TN: Abingdon Press, 2003.

Wagner, Peter. *Engaging the Enemy*. Ventura, CA: Regal Books, 1991.

Warren, Rick. *The Purpose-Driven Church: Growth Without Compromising Your Message and Mission*. Grand Rapids, MI: Zondervan, 1995.

Wilkes, Gene. *Jesus on Leadership*. Wheaton, IL: Tyndale House Publishing, 1998.

Williams, Angie. *Jesus Wants Your Mind*. Kearney, NE: Morris Publishing, 2012.

Wood, Gene. *Leading Turnaround Churches*. St. Charles, IL: Churchsmart Resources, 2001.

Yancey, Philip. Church: *Why Bother?* Grand Rapids, MI: Zondervan, 1998.

Yohannan, K. P. *Revolution in World Missions*. Carrollton, TX: gfa books, a division of Gospel for Asia, 1986; 38th printing 2011.

Yun, Brother. *Living Water.* Grand Rapids, MI: Zondervan, 2008.